TO THE
ENDS OF
THE
EARTH

TO THE ENDS OF THE EARTH

HUGH STEVEN

CHRISTIAN HERALD BOOKS
Chappaqua, New York

TO THE ENDS OF THE EARTH

INTRODUCTION

All I had to show for six weeks of hedge-hopping over a country that wouldn't stop was a cloth bag filled with twenty hours of cassette tapes, two stenographer's notebooks filled with personal comments and observations, and twenty-five rolls of exposed color film.

But the sights and sounds and smells of Brazil are etched forever in my mind. How could one ever forget the unending forests, the Amazon River that is more like a sea than a river, the everchanging hues of green, the late afternoon sun glinting off the swamps, and aquatic fern like a gigantic carpet of diamonds.

But my most profound memories are the memories of people—Wycliffe Bible Translators from around the world, all working as one body for one cause in one geographic location. Some were translators, some pilots, some homemakers. There were community developers, short term helpers, maintenance people, managers of centers, linguistic, literacy and Bible translation consultants, radio operators, carpenters, teachers, and, of course, the children.

Some were expecting their first child. Others were sending older children back to the United States for schooling and were concerned for their spiritual well-being. Some were second-generation Wycliffe workers; others were being stationed for the first time and were filled with awe at their responsibilities.

Each one was beautiful, unique—a part of the body. It was evident that God had worked and was at work, building, molding each into the image of his Son, Jesus.

I could have written a story about any one of them, but under what I believe to be the leading of the Spirit I have chosen four families—the Greens, Grahams, Sheldons, and Koehns—to represent not the whole but a cross-section of what God has done through Wycliffe in Brazil during these past twenty years.

In these four families there is an interface of suffering and crises.

Without understanding why, and in most cases without questioning why, each knew intuitively that the highest things in life are gained only through struggle. It follows then, that suffering is an essential part of life, growth and maturity.

Here then are four vignettes of families who, through obedience and struggle, are gaining *to agathon* of life—the highest good.

The Observer

BRAZIL

VENEZUELA

GUYANA

COLOMBIA

FRENCH
GUIANA

SURINAM

MAKUSI

PALIKUR

KARIPUNA

APALAI OIAMPI

MAKÚ

HIXKARYÁNA

BELÉM

MANAUS▲

ASURINÍ URUBÚ SÃO LUIZ

SATERÉ

MUNDURUKÚ

GUAJAJÁRA

CANELA

APINAYÉ

DENÍ

TÚMA

JAMAMADÍ

PAUMARÍ

APURINÃ

MÚRA-PIRAHÃ

PARINTINTÍN

RECIFE

▲PORTO VELHO

KARITIÁNA

KAYAPÓ

RIKBAKTSA

KARAJÁ

SURUÍ

CINTA-LARGA

KAYABÍ

KAMAYURÁ

WAURÁ

MAMAINDÉ

NAMBIKUÁRA

PARECÍS

XAVÁNTE

BAKAIRÍ

SALVADOR

CUIABÁ▲

BOLIVIA

BORÔRO

BRASÍLIA▲

MAXAKALÍ

KADIWÉU

TERÉNA

BELO HORIZONTE

KAIWÁ

PARAGUAY

SÃO PAULO

RIO DE JANEIRO

GUARÁNI

KAINGÁNG

ARGENTINA

PORTO ALEGRE

URUGUAY

PERU

RIO BRANCO

Chapter One

My name is Leon. It has been more than ten years since the Old Ones (we call those we respect by this name) and their two baby sons came to live among my people, the Palikúrs. They built their house next door to mine and since neither of our homes had walls, we became well acquainted. Later, when they learned to speak my language, *Senhor* Harold told me that our country, Brazil, is different from his country. But he said there is a part of his country called the Everglades that is very much like our land. The big difference, he said, is that the Everglades are in the southern part of his country while our scattered jungle islands and marshlands are on the northern coast of Brazil.

Senhor Harold told me there are many kinds of birds, lizards, alligators and deer in the Everglades as there are here. I do not understand why they do not hunt monkeys and tapir and piranha fish as we do. Perhaps it is because all his people live in big cities like Brasilia and Rio de Janeiro and Saõ Paulo. Yet his son—the one they call Timmy—is a mighty fisherman, worthy of being called a Palikúr. He once caught over a thousand piranha fish in three months, using only a little strip of colored cloth fastened onto a small hook—so different from our sons who use spears and bows and arrows.

Ah, but I have told you too much too soon. Let me go back to the day they first came in their small canoe to our village.

I told you my name, but I didn't tell you that I used to be a witch doctor. As a young boy I was taught the secret songs which were sung when someone became sick because of an evil animal spirit. If someone had a swollen stomach, I knew the spirit of a snake had entered in. Other symptoms were caused by the spirit of a deer or a tapir, a sloth or a jaguar. No matter what sickness it was, I could determine which spirit had entered the body by simply looking at a person and feeling him all over. I would then either blow tobacco smoke over him, or sing the right song. Sometimes I needed to draw the spirit out by sucking on the area that seemed sorest. I always pulled out a stone or a little stick and told the person that he was cured. Sometimes it worked, other times I knew the sickness was beyond my power. That is what happened the day the Old Ones first came—the night the village people brought the young woman to me.

"I have come for help," said the woman's mother. "It has been two days since my daughter's first child came. My daughter still bleeds. Do what you must. Blow over her, sing over her, pass your rattle over her. She will die if you do not help."

I had seen many women who had problems with their first baby, but this was the worst. She had lost too much blood. She was cold and no longer spoke or responded. I saw at once there was no hope.

"Why don't you ask for help from the white woman who has come to live among us?" I said.

"Who are those people?" asked the mother of the sick woman. "It is not our custom to welcome outsiders. Why have they come here?"

"They are from a land far away called the United States," I said. "They say the reason they have come is to tell us about Father God."

"All Palikúrs know there is a god," the mother said, "but no one knows his dwelling place or how to talk to him."

"Since they have come to tell us about God," I said, "perhaps the white woman would ask him to help your daughter."

I must tell you I suggested this, not so much to help the woman's daughter (I knew she would die), but to see what the white woman would do. Did her god have more power than I? I was indeed to be surprised.

I watched without speaking as she climbed the steep ladder from the ground to the floor of my house. We Palikúrs build our houses high above the ground on long poles. We have learned from our fathers that this is the best way. It keeps us dry when rains swell the rivers.

When the white woman saw the sick stranger, she simply touched her. Then she bowed her head and said something in her own language. She didn't chant, or whistle or hum. She didn't even blow smoke over her.

Then she did something very strange. She wept. This woman, called Diana, who could not yet speak our language and was not yet one of us, wept because one Palikúr was going to die. She also tried to say something

to the sick woman's mother. The mother did not understand, nor did I, but the words were soft and said in
kindness.

After the Old One left, the mother took the young
woman away, and I lay on my sleeping mat thinking.
Could anyone talk with God? I wondered. I knew he
was our Creator, but he lived so far away. He would not
be interested in one little Palikúr woman who did not
know how to stop her bleeding after her baby had come.
Besides, it was too late for him to do anything for this
girl *if* he could. No, God was not interested in us. We
lived too far away for him to care.

That ended my thinking for that day. I knew the
young woman would die. For several days I listened for
the death wail, but heard none. To my great amazement, I learned that this woman, who I knew must die,
grew stronger. Only God could have done such a thing.

A few weeks after this young woman was healed, I
again saw God's power. This time it was not the problem
of sickness—it was the problem of demons! A family
had brought me their daughter who was screaming and
speaking horrible, vile language that Palikúr men do
not speak even in private. She was wild! With foam
coming from her mouth, she kicked and shook. No one
could stop her.

I did not know what to do, so I called to the white
man, called Harold.

"Here is a girl controlled by evil spirits," I said as
Senhor Harold climbed up the ladder. Then as I had
when the woman Diana came in, I watched in curious

silence. Again I was greatly surprised. For all this man did was speak softly, but with strength, to the girl, and immediately the girl was quiet. Later I learned he had asked God's Son, Jesus, to drive out the evil spirit.

Now when I saw these things, I knew God was very great. He could not be far away, and indeed man could talk with him. It was then I decided to watch closely what these strange outsiders did. And because I wanted to learn more from them, I, with other Palikúrs, helped them learn our language and helped them cut the long poles for their house. But I never stopped watching how they lived their lives each day.

What I saw made me wonder how it was that God could work through them, but did not always protect them. One day I helped *Senhor* Harold move into his new house. That day he slipped and fell on top of a canoe and broke his rib. Also, both *Senhor* Harold and his wife, *Dona* Diana, suffered much from fever and chills of malaria—just as we Palikúrs do.

I was later told that *Senhor* Harold almost died from this malaria. Yet even though I wondered why his God did not care for them in these matters, I knew they were different people, different from any who had ever come to our land.

Take the way *Senhor* Harold walked. He could walk fast but not as most men. He told me something about having cerebral palsy. It came to him from an injury when he was born. But no matter. When the men of the village hunted or fished, he walked without complaint. He never asked them to walk slower when they raced

ahead in the excitement of a kill. He was more interested in spending time with us so that he could learn
our language than killing the game.

I thought this strange, and one day I told him my
thoughts. *Senhor* Harold smiled. He said he and his wife
had waited eighteen long months before they had been
given permission to live among us. All that time they
had prayed that we Palikúr people would grow hungry
to know God and desire to read his Words.

Then he said he was trying to make up for lost time.
This I did not understand. How could time be lost? We
have so much of it! What did it matter if some were lost?
Then *Senhor* Harold taught us again about Jesus Christ,
God's Son. "Jesus can bring you into contact with our
Father God," he said.

I was pleased to hear this, as were many others of our
village. We Palikúrs have a song that asks a question no
one had ever been able to answer.

> "Where will I go when I die?
> Will I go to a barren rock
> In the midst of an endless sea?"

Maybe the Old Ones could answer these questions.

Most in our village grew to love the Old Ones. They
continued to surprise us with their goodness. Not that
they were stronger or knew more than we did. *Senhor*
Harold could never cut house poles, or fish, and hunt
like a Palikúr man! But somehow that did not matter.
People began to say, "These Old Ones know all about
God and we want to learn. We want to know all there is
to know about Jesus. No one has ever told us anything
like this before."

I even laughed a little when an old man, who sat listening to what *Senhor* Harold called a gospel recording, would not go home. It was far into the night and *Senhor* Harold, who wanted to find rest for his eyes, hinted for him to leave. But the old man shook his head and said, "Who can sleep when they have a chance to hear news like this!"

And I remember a man who kept asking the Old Ones if the book of God were ready for us to read. When the Old Ones answered *no,* he said, "Then I wish you would teach me about Jesus every morning, every noon, and every night. I want so much to have a clean heart." I did not feel as strongly as he; I did not see that I was a terrible sinner.

Even though I liked the Old Ones and the words they spoke, I did not feel I needed to change my ways. After all, I was the witch doctor. Who else knew the secrets of our people and would be able to pass them on to our children?

One day I talked with Paulo. He had been given the words of God in Portuguese by a man who believed and obeyed the same way as the Old Ones. Paulo spent much more time with the Old Ones than I did, so I asked him what he thought about this Jesus.

"My heart is open," said Paulo, "and Jesus has given me a new way of thinking."

That is all he said, and I still did not understand. But then two things happened that made me want this new way.

The first happened when one of *Senhor* Harold's helpers took his motor without permission. When the Old Ones were out of the village, this man shamelessly took the motor, attached it to his canoe and went to visit another island. But this man did not understand the secrets of such a machine and the importance of the liquids called oil and gasoline.

When the man returned, it was with great fear. The motor's smoke was blue and black and was as *Senhor* Harold later said, "burned out." Like all of us, the man expected to be greeted with hot words. It was the Old One's right to be angry. Instead, *Senhor* Harold forgave him and was gracious and loving to this man. Never in our history had such a thing happened. It is still something we talk about around the night fires.

The night after this happened, we men of the village sat by a night fire, close to the smoke which drove away the mosquitoes. We told and retold the story of the motor and after each telling, a man named Davi would say, "*Senhor* Harold is like Shinuwa—without anger. It is just as Shinuwa told us to be—kind and generous and peaceful."

You see, a strange event happened to this Palikúr man called Shinuwa when Davi and I were boys.

The man named Shinuwa died. In those days it was our custom to split open the body, clean out the insides, and roast the corpse so it would not decay. Then we kept it in a large clay pot until we wanted to bury it.

The people were just about to open Shinuwa, when all of a sudden he sat up—alive! An amazing thing had happened to him, but it was not until four years later that he told us about it. All who knew Shinuwa during those four years watched him because he had become kinder and more generous—and never showed anger.

Finally Shinuwa gathered us together and told us

why. "When I died, I had a vision. I dreamed I was walking up a long road toward God. Off to the side was a fire and I thought I heard people in the fire screaming. After I walked a while, a man stopped me. 'You can't go any further unless you have a pass,' he said. I didn't know I needed a pass to go to God. I began to cry. I wanted so much to go to God, but I didn't have a pass.

"Then the man said, 'I am sorry. You must go back and get a pass to come here to God.'

"It was then I woke up. Since that time I have thought much about God and now I want to tell you about him. The reason I could not go to him was because God is so good and I am so bad. Listen to me! God wants us to honor him. He doesn't want us to be angry at each other or steal or kill. He wants us to be good like he is."

We all heard these words and were touched in our hearts and decided to be good. We tried very hard, but after a while we were just as bad as ever. We didn't know what to think of Shinuwa's words. But when the Old Ones came to us and I helped them put God's Word into my language. I learned that Jesus said, "I am the way, the truth, and the life!" I knew that Jesus was the way to God. He was our pass!

When we understood this, we knew by his power we could be what he wanted us to be. We knew that God cared for us, that he wanted us to be his, and that he reached out to us, so far away from him, to bring us to himself.

In the beginning I told you I watched how the Old Ones lived. I was impressed that they lived each day as Shinuwa had said God wanted Palikúrs to live. Therefore, seeing how powerful their God was, I decided one day to speak to the Old Ones about these things.

"Please," I said to them, "please teach me to pray so that I can get God to do what I want him to do." To this day I smile when I think of that request. The Old Ones just looked at each other. Then *Senhor* Harold said, "We don't pray to God to get him to do what we want. We pray so that we can do what *God* wants."

This was so strange to me. I wanted the power they had so I could heal the sick that came to me. WhenI told the Old Ones this, they began to teach me more about Jesus. They said God loved me, that he wanted me and all people to become like his Son, Jesus.

I have already told you that I thought I was pretty good and didn't need to change. But as the Old Ones taught me day by day, I began to see I wasn't as good as I had thought. What shocked me the most was the story of how the people killed Jesus and how he said, "Father, forgive them." I knew I could never do a thing like that—no Palikúr could. It was our custom to revenge anyone who was killed by another man.

Another thing that bothered me was that I got drunk all the time and this made me do things I shouldn't.

Most people from the outside do not understand how a Palikúr man feels deep in his heart. At first we thought the storeman understood. He sold us our whiskey. When our women wanted food or a piece of cloth he told us, "No. It is better to drink this whiskey." And when we all became drunk, we forgot the hard days of our lives. Forgetting was better than living.

Perhaps this is why when the Old Ones came and told us about God's love, we listened.

One day as I lay on my sleeping mat thinking of all I had seen and all the Old Ones had told me, I saw how bad my drunkenness was. And I began to talk to God. I asked him to take away my badness and put his Spirit in me. I began to feel as if my heart were wrapped in green scum from the swamp. And I let him take my sin and he did! And then because I had been "lifted up" by Jesus, I said, "Now, God, I just want to do what You want me to."

Since then I have continued to help the sick, but not in the same way I used to. Now I pray for them and God makes them well. I don't sing the witch doctor songs anymore because God has given me new songs to sing—songs about him. He gives me so many songs, I teach them to everyone else so all together we can praise God.

There are many other things I want to tell you but I will first tell you how the Old Ones learned to be one of us.

Chapter Two

It was in January 1965 that we Palikúrs welcomed *Senhor* Harold, *Dona* Diana, and their two young sons, Timmy and David. They said they had come to learn our language, but they had many other things to learn first. They had never tasted alligator or lizard.

Dona Diana slowly learned the ways of our Palikúr women. At first she did not understand why our women run to the river and wash when one of them has given birth to twins. They believe that this washing will keep them from also having twins.

Before the other Palikúrs and I were "lifted up by Jesus," we did many other things the Old Ones did not understand. I think it made them sad to see us drink so much at our parties. We would fill a dugout canoe full of fermented manioc juice and drink it until the canoe was empty. And could we dance! Children, old men, everyone! We would dance to the drumbeats until we could no longer stand. Then we would look for a place to lie down until we were sober again.

But although it made them sad to see us drunk, they were still kind to us and always willing to talk with us. After one party when many of us were drunk, we went to visit them. I overheard one of my people say, "I live

25

waiting for the Book of God. I want to know what God's Book says." And I heard several of the Palikúr leaders say they too were interested.

I have already told you some stories about the Old Ones, but I have not yet told you how they were once lost a whole night in the Atlantic Ocean in a tiny dugout canoe.

They had been with us three months when they left to go back to the city. The morning was bright and clear as they climbed into their new fifteen-foot dugout canoe that one of my people had made for them. *Senhor* Harold sat in the back so that he could run their small outboard motor; *Dona* Diana sat ahead of him with two-year-old Timmy at her side and ten-month-old David in her arms. They waved good-by to those of us gathered on the bank and soon we could no longer see them.

Dona Diana said she warned Timmy to keep his hands out of the water. "They may get nibbled by a paranha!" she said.

For two hours they all relaxed and enjoyed the trip. Suddenly, without warning, the river ahead was completely clogged with wide-leafed plants. It seemed there was no end to them and there did not seem to be any way to get through them. The motor stopped and by the time *Senhor* Harold got it started again, they were completely surrounded by the plants.

"What will we do?" said *Dona* Diana.

"First we're going to pray for guidance," said *Senhor* Harold. And do you know when they raised their heads after praying they heard the sound of another motor! It was the government Indian agent for the area. This was a miracle because he was practically the only man who traveled the river at that point and he did so only a few times a year.

He helped the Old Ones get untangled from the plants and showed them how to pole into the marshlands which bordered the river. The Old Ones thanked him for his help and continued on their way while the Indian agent continued his journey in the other direction.

At noon they reached the government Indian Post where they had made arrangements for an experienced Brazilian to guide them around the well-named Mosquito Point. There they would leave the Uacá River on which they were traveling, sail across a bay which opened to the Atlantic Ocean, and enter the Oiapoque River. This was a dangerous part of their journey. Many boats larger than their canoe had been lost in the choppy waves and twelve-foot-high tidal bores.

The man who was to be their guide through the difficult waters had been called away unexpectedly. The only person available to go with them was his fourteen-year-old son.

"Are you sure he is able to guide us through?" asked *Senhor* Harold.

"Yes, yes," said the boy's mother. "Do not be afraid. My boy is experienced."

The Old Ones had no choice but to take him. "We will travel at night," said the boy. "There is less wind then and the water is calmer. Don't worry. Nothing can go wrong."

They left with the tide at 8 P.M. Their young guide sat at the prow of the canoe shining a flashlight in the direction *Senhor* Harold was to steer. They traveled this way for many hours. The quarter-moon disappeared. Fog nearly blotted out the stars. It was still and black.

Suddenly the canoe ran full speed into a mud bank and stopped dead.

"What happened?" asked *Dona* Diana. "Where are we?"

"I don't know," said *Senhor* Harold, "but I think our guide fell asleep."

There was no land to be seen and had the mud bank not stopped them, they might have kept going on out into open sea!

After much effort they were able to get free of the mud and *Senhor* Harold tried to decide what to do. "I think we'd better turn left," said the young guide. They did, but a little later when he said turn left again, *Senhor* Harold became worried. When the boy repeated the command several more times, the Old Ones became alarmed.

"Diana," said *Senhor* Harold, "I've been watching those few stars. I believe we've made three circles in this bay!"

Now the Old Ones began to wonder if they would ever set foot on land again. The ocean waves rose to within three inches of the edge of their boat. *Dona* Diana said later she was sure they were going to drown. "Help us, Lord," she prayed, as she pushed away the thought of her family gasping in the water.

And the Lord heard her and understood her fears of the water and said, "What does it matter how or when you die? What is important is the village of people you left behind. Are they never going to learn to live?"

Then *Dona* Diana showed how much love she had for my people, because she was no longer concerned for her safety but began to understand how much God loved the Palikúrs. She felt God would save them because he had brought them to live among us that we might hear of him. "It doesn't matter what happens to us," she prayed, "but the Palikúrs need You so much. If we don't make it, Lord, send someone, send someone to give them your Word."

Just as she finished praying, the young guide shouted in relief, "I see land! Go straight ahead!"

"I'm not sure that's a good idea," *Senhor* Harold exclaimed. "There are bound to be rocks along the shore." But it was too late. They were already surrounded by jagged rocks that stuck up from the dark water like gigantic teeth.

"We'll capsize if we hit those rocks!" *Senhor* Harold shouted as he frantically pulled in the motor. Then there was a sickening crunch and the canoe was wedged tightly between two rocks. There, lost, with angry waves splashing into their tiny dugout and rain pelting them, they were safe. They could not turn over. The Old Ones said they felt the rocks were the hands of God. No matter where they were, they were safe in his hands.

It was impossible to free themselves. They would have to wait for the tide to come in and lift them up. *Senhor*

Harold insisted *Dona* Diana try to sleep. She took her two little boys, lay down on top of two packed duffle bags and fell asleep—rain and all!

A few hours later, the water began to rise, and the canoe began to slam against the rocks. *Senhor* Harold cautiously paddled away, got the motor started, only to have it stop—they had hit another mud bank! This meant more waiting for the tide to free them and by now the wind was blowing hard and the waves were growing higher and higher. *Senhor* Harold got the motor started again, but they had more trouble—the twenty-foot docking rope had been washed overboard and was tangled in the propeller.

Senhor Harold had to lean out over the water to cut it away with a knife and all the while the waves lifted and dropped, lifted and dropped the canoe. *Senhor* Harold's face began to grow pale.

He had not been feeling too well after a severe attack of malaria and the broken rib, and now that the motor was free, he found he was too weak to run it.

"I'll run it," said their young guide. "I know how."

The Old Ones had their doubts but there was nothing else they could do. Confidently the young guide climbed to the rear of the canoe and turned the motor on full throttle. Vrooom! Immediately the canoe filled with water. *Dona* Diana bailed as quickly as she could and yelled for the boy to slow down. But Harold, as sick as he was, didn't wait to see what other trouble the boy could get into. He grabbed the steering handle from him and took over. Things were under control again.

alikur children. Poling a canoe through the marsh.

Satere woman and her child.

A Satere family traveling the river.

Cleaning fish.

A Satere teenager.

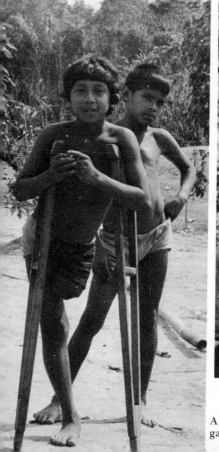

Servo, Al Graham's co-translator,
friend and first convert.

A Satere boy, who lost his leg from
gangrene that set in after snake bite.

Sharpening a knife on a whetstone.

Ed Koehn in Bona (his village)
receiving a gift of fruit from an Apalai man.

Sally Koehn.

Ed opens a new outboard motor, and explains how it works to two Apalai men.

An Apalai boy at the entrance to a hut.

An Apalai girl.

Jaques' son.

Jaques, an Apalai Indian,
the Koehn's friend and co-translator.

Well, not quite. They ran out of gas, and even after they filled up with the extra gas they had on board, the motor still refused to go. *Senhor* Harold tried to clean the valves, which was difficult in the choppy water. He got the motor started again and everything was fine, except for one small point. The battered canoe had sprung a leak. While *Senhor* Harold safely guided his family to their destination, *Dona* Diana had to constantly bail to keep the canoe from filling with water. As the sun began to rise, they noticed that the splashing waves no longer tasted salty. They were in the Oiapoque River. It should only have taken them an hour to round Mosquito Point. Instead it had taken them a whole night!

When we talked of their adventure later, they said, "That night will always be a reminder to us that God will be with us no matter what the problem, danger, darkness or barrier. It will encourage us that, no matter what we face, God's message will still be told. And it is a promise to us that we will reach our goal because it is his goal and we are in his hands."

If you were to ask the Old Ones if they had any other experience that year that compared with this, they would say no. Yet they talk frequently about two other days: the day *Dona* Diana found four poisonous snakes in their bedroom, and the day they found Timmy sailing down river with three of his little friends in a flimsy canoe. (They were able to rescue him and hoped that next time he would wait for his daddy to take him for a boat ride!)

My people soon learned that the Old Ones wanted to

help us. For this reason we wanted to make *Senhor* Harold chief. He said he could not accept but we could see it pleased him that we wanted him for this important position in the village.

Before they came, many of our people died of disease, but the second year they were among us, only two died. One day, in a heavy rainstorm, a woman who was dying of pneumonia came three hours in a canoe to get medicine. We all thought she would die, but she got well. We were surprised when *Senhor* Harold gave her his jacket to wear back to her home. "It will protect you from the rain," he said.

I felt sad when the Old Ones suffered with malaria attacks. But this never stopped them from learning about us. They recorded many stories about our Palikúr culture. They said it was to help them learn our language.

In their third year with us the first Palikúrs began to understand about the God the Old Ones came to tell us about. By then the Old Ones could speak our language well and many of us began to ask more and more questions. It seemed as if something inside us was crying out to know this true God.

Paulo was the first to be "lifted up by Jesus." He did not keep quiet about it but told many others how they could be "untied" and "lifted up." Before long, eight Palikúrs believed.

When the Old Ones first came to my island, there were only three families living here. Now those who had believed in Jesus wanted to move near the Old Ones to learn more about this great God. The Old Ones left that year to go to their own country for a long stay, and when they returned, eleven families had moved to my island—all of us Christians and all of us telling others on other islands about Jesus.

When the Old Ones were gone away from us to their own land, their house burned down. God was good to see that their language material was saved. The house burned so hot it melted the water pump into a lump.

When they returned, the Old Ones did not stay long as they wanted to go to their Belém Center to translate the first seven chapters of Mark, the Life of Christ and an alphabet book.

The following year when they came to live with us again we helped *Senhor* Harold clear land for the coming of the "Sky Canoe." It was a happy day when they no longer had to make the long canoe trip.

Dona Diana spent her time caring for our sick. She helped us understand that we could trust God to heal our sick and we began to see it was he who made them well.

She told us to wash our hands before eating. "You will have less dysentery and worms if you do." We also did not know we should give God thanks for our food before eating. We learned to do this much faster than washing our hands! *Dona* Diana did not get too upset with us, "Because," she said, "God works from the inside out."

Many other things happened to show us the power of the Living God. Before the Old Ones came, we Palikúrs worshiped the power of the moon. At night we sang to the moon like this:

> Moon, we worship you.
> We watch in wonder at your
>   mysterious power.
> Night after night we see the
>   darkness slowly eat you up
> Until nothing but silver
>   remains.
> Then suddenly you reappear,
>   full and glowing.
> O Moon, what is the secret
> Of your power to live again?

We worshiped the moon because we feared death. To us the moon was a symbol of new life—something we could never attain. But now all those fears are gone. Miraculously, life has been given to us—new life that begins right now and never ends. This life is in Jesus Christ.

It was not long after we in our village had begun to trust Jesus that the oldest woman among the Palikúrs died. She was the last living member of the Sun Clan who we believed had given us our language long ago. She was also one of the first to become a Christian.

Early one morning she came to us all and said simply, "Today I am going to see Jesus." She didn't seem to be ill and we didn't understand her. At midday she said again, "I'm so happy. I'm going to see Jesus." That evening she died, not in fear, but with a smile and with the words, "Now I am going to see Jesus."

Let me tell you two more stories of how God has changed our thinking about death.

Not long after the old woman died, another woman died. And some began the old death wail. One of the woman's married daughters fell to the floor crying hysterically. The loss of her mother was too great for her to bear. But suddenly in the middle of her grief, the daughter stopped crying and sat up.

With a look of great amazement on her face, she said, "Jesus just spoke to me. He told me not to act like this. My old mother has gone to be with Jesus. She is happy there. She won't suffer any more. Therefore I should not be sad. I should be happy. It is selfish to want her back here."

We are now not afraid of death as we once were. But there is something else. When we die we want to be clean and ready to meet Jesus our Savior—the One who has lifted us up and untied us. I will now tell you my second story. It is about a young man named Masawyan.

A few months ago this young man had a dream. In it someone resembling an angel told him he would soon sleep. He interpreted this to mean he was going to die. When he told us, he said, "If I die, it doesn't matter, but you all keep going on with God." We couldn't understand why he talked this way. He was strong and without sickness. Besides, the Lord was using him in our village. Masawyan could not preach very well or share about Jesus in church like the others. Instead, each day he would gather the children of the village together and teach them all our songs about Jesus. This was his work for the Lord.

The day after his dream, the Lord showed him some things that were not right in his life. When the Lord did this, Masawyan went around to each of us and confessed any sins he had committed against us—sins like being angry or gossiping. That evening he came to visit me. "I'm so happy," he said, "that I can't eat or sleep. Let us sing some songs." So we sang songs about the Lord almost all night long.

The next day we all went out to help a brother clear his field. While we were chopping down some of the trees, one of the trees fell on Masawyan. It split open his skull and he died instantly. We felt terrible about this, but knew it was not just an accident. God had already known about it, and he had let Masawyan know about it too so he would be ready to meet him.

Masawyan's death didn't leave us with fear and terror and hopeless sorrowing as it would have done before. No one started the death wail. Instead we began to think about putting away anything in our lives that would keep us from being ready to meet Jesus. We mourned for our brother because we would miss him, but we also searched our hearts to make everything right in our lives that was wrong. We agreed that we must not begin to give the devil a place in our minds.

If someone lies to us or wrongs us in other ways, we should not spend our time thinking about how he has sinned against us. Rather we should turn our attention to Jesus, think his thoughts and praise him. All of us knew it could have been any of us who were hit by that tree. We all wanted to be as ready as Masawyan had been!

But not all my Palikúr brothers were happy with this new way of thinking. Some refused to listen and said it was wrong because our fathers and grandfathers did not believe this way. One of these was Setwel and I will tell you about him now.

Chapter Three

For many years Setwel was one of the best witch doctors among the Palikúrs—even better than I. He knew the songs for all the animal spirits and remembered everything his grandfather taught him about curing the sick and casting curses on people, as I did.

When he first heard that God had a Son who came to earth because he loved him, Setwel said, "I don't want to hear about him. I cannot believe this. I have never heard this before. I work to get spirits *out* of people. Why do you speak of letting God put his Spirit *into* them? I do not want to be under God's control. I want to do things my way—the old way."

I and other Palikúr witch doctors tried to tell him that even though we had once thought as he, Jesus had untied us and given us a new way of thinking. But he refused to listen.

Then one day his wife who was much younger than he said, "Husband, I want to go to the place where Leon and the others who believe in Jesus sing and read from the paper that tells what Jesus said."

"No!" said Setwel. "No, you can't go!"

His young wife begged and begged him to let her go, but he still said, "No!"

After a while Setwel thought his wife had lost interest as she no longer asked permission to go to the meetings. She *had* lost interest in Jesus. At the same time she had become interested in another man—a man much closer to her age. She wanted to be free of Setwel but was afraid to leave because she thought he might curse her.

One day when Setwel wasn't suspecting anything, she sneaked up behind him and began beating him with a canoe paddle.

"Don't kill me! For God's sake don't kill me!" Setwel cried.

"What do I know about God?" said his wife. "Nothing! And that is no one's fault but yours." Then she stopped beating Setwel and ran away.

Setwel was badly wounded and that is when I and my Christian brothers came to help him—the very ones he would not allow into his house! We brought him food and asked what we could do for him.

This surprised Setwel but not as much as the visit from a man whom he had cursed some months before. When this Christian man had learned of the curse he showed no fear. "Jesus will protect me," he said. Setwel was amazed that Jesus did just that. The man did not get sick.

But after thinking awhile, this Christian man became angry with Setwel for cursing him and he in turn cursed Setwel. And did Setwel get sick! So sick he thought he was going to die. When this Christian man heard that Setwel was sick, he saw his sin and went to Setwel. "I was wrong to curse you," said the Christian man. "Please forgive me." Then he prayed for Setwel to get well. This was all very strange to Setwel, even stranger when he quickly became well.

Now as Setwel lay suffering from his wife's beating he had time to think about all that had happened. He knew it was not normal for a man to ask forgiveness. The man should have been happy that Setwel got sick. Setwel began to wonder if this was the kind of thing men do when they have God's Spirit in them. He suddenly began to realize that if he had allowed his wife to know God like she had wanted to she would never have beaten him. "Why, oh why didn't I let her go to the meetings? Why didn't I listen?" he said.

As he lay on his sleeping mat day after day, he became weaker and weaker. He knew he was dying. He told us he was having horrible visions of demons coming to get him. Then his daughter came to take him down river to her village. But before he left, he called all the people of the village together.

"You were right," he said. "I should have listened to you when you told me about Jesus. Now it is too late for me."

"No," we said. "It is never too late, Setwel. You can yet know God. You can have contact with our heavenly Father through Jesus Christ. You can still let God put his Spirit in you!"

"No," said Setwel, "I want to, but I just cannot. It is too late now, too late."

We could not convince him and Setwel went away, never to return to that village.

But Setwel's life did not end without hope. Before he died, God caused Setwel to have a dream. In that dream he saw a large book in which were written all the names of everyone from his old village who were going to heaven. Setwel looked and looked but he could not find his name written in that book.

Setwel was at last without pride and said, "Lord, I am no good, but You are. Please write my name in your Book." And God did. Before Setwel died people said he rejoiced in his salvation and was joyful to be untied and lifted up by Jesus.

Five years after the Old Ones came to live among us, we Palikúr Christians met for the first time to remember how Jesus died for us. The Old Ones provided purple "Kool-Aid" and crackers for our Good Friday evening communion service.

We did not work that day. We spent our time listening to gospel recordings of songs and sermons in our language. The next day we had another service. We used the booklet "The Life of Christ" which *Senhor* Harold had translated for us.

"These are very good words," we told him.

I need to mention our "Celebration Service" held June 15, 1970. Fifteen of my people read from the "Life of Christ" booklet. What was special about that? Why, only a few short years before that time most of us had never held a book in our hands! Now we were reading our own Palikúr language for the first time. (As you say in your language—our excitement was so high we had butterflies in our insides.) We had spent two months in a reading course and graduated. Ten others almost finished the course and they were given honorable mention.

Dona Diana gave each of us who had completed the course a new book in our language and a cake. Some of us had never eaten cake before, so it was a special treat. "This cake is a reminder for you," said *Dona* Diana. "Just as we eat each day for physical growth and strength, we must read the Bible each day for spiritual growth and strength. As the cake is sweet, so is God's Word sweet to our souls."

Paulo, the first Christian, was now our pastor. He encouraged us to "teach others also." Then he noticed that large black ants had crawled over some of the cakes, so he added, "This cake will soon disappear, but nothing can take God's Word from your hearts and lives. If you read his Word, you are laying up treasure in heaven that neither moth, nor rust, nor ANTS can destroy!"

Our lives have certainly changed. At night, instead of getting drunk, we Palikúr men meet around a campfire to tell what God has taught us that day. If you come by our houses in the daytime, you will hear us encouraging and praying with each other.

We have built our own Palikúr church on my island because there are so many of us living here. This is new for us because before we did not like to live that close together. But now we are bound together by our love for the Lord.

Each year *Senhor* Harold has given us more and more of God's Word as Davi has helped him put it into our language. How we love the Word! Some of us memorize whole chapters.

We have our own evangelistic team. Paulo takes fourteen men and they visit many neighboring villages to spread the Good News. We all meet in the church when they return to hear what happened.

"In one house there was a very sick man," reported one member of the evangelistic team. "His wife told us he was sick in the head. He had been climbing up the posts of his house and swinging from the rafters. Finally he became exhausted and had fallen. When we saw him, he was too weak to sit up. Then he saw us and said, 'When I heard you were coming, I was happy. I knew Jesus was coming with you.' We prayed for the man right there, and not for him only, but for all the people, that their hearts would be healed. Right away the man got up, sat down, and asked us to tell him more about Jesus. When the people saw this they said, 'Now we know God is with you.'"

I have not yet told you that a few years ago the Old Ones were thought by the government to have hidden a gold mine. Some soldiers broke into their home, searching for the canoe-loads of gold they were supposed to have. But they could not find them. This caused the government to make a thorough investigation of them and they were able to announce that the rumor was false.

God used this experience to make the Old Ones translate harder and the Palikúr Christians pray harder. Oh yes, and the government had more confidence in the Old Ones than ever. You see how all things worked together for good!

I have told you that we Palikúrs learned to read, but I have not told you we also learned to write. Not just words, but whole stories! My friend Moses, a Palikúr

Christian, is the best. He has written ten easy reading books and a one-page phrase book for Palikúrs to learn Portuguese. One of his books is about the angels' announcement of Jesus' birth. When he checked it over he said, "The angels didn't tell the smart people, or the rich people—they were asleep. They told the poor shepherds who were awake and watching."

The Old Ones have not only taught many of us to read while they have translated God's Good Words, they have also made many songs and hymns for us to sing. One day a former medicine man wanted to obey Colossians 3:16 which says (in Palikúr):

> Grab hold of Christ's words well in your hearts. Teach and advise one another with all God's wisdom, with songs that call upon God and honor God. Sing with God's Spirit. Sing songs praising God with all your hearts.

But this man had a problem. He thought he could not use Palikúr music (that we had used with our drinking and dancing) to sing praises to God. The only other music he knew was the music the Old Ones used for their songs and hymns, and he couldn't make songs with that.

Then the Old Ones said, "Your music is given to you by God just as your language is. You can use your words for good or evil, and you can use your music for good or evil. The Lord wants the Palikúrs to praise Him with their music just as they do with their language."

The man was happy and the Lord then gave this man some new words to an old song which formerly said, "I

am a devil-one." He changed it to, "I am a Jesus-one."
This song touched our hearts and many others began to
put new words to other old melodies. In three months
over 70 new songs were written by 23 different people—old and young, men and women! One man said,
"Long ago we sang for our pleasure. Now we sing for
God's pleasure and at the same time it comforts us."

When the Old Ones asked one woman which songs
she liked best—those they had made or those with
Palikúr tunes, she replied, "They are both pretty. I like
them both, but the Palikúr music can make me cry." We
share her feelings and often say, "Adahan kadni*ka*."
"(These songs) make you feel *deeply*."

Remember how before the Old Ones came we used to
sing a song about a barren rock? One day after I had a
dream, I put new words to this song. I told the village, "I
dreamed I was on a great glittering white rock. My
enemies were shooting at me but couldn't reach me. I
realized the rock was Jesus. The Lord gave me new
words to that old song. Now we can sing about our
Rock, Jesus Christ."

Yes, because the Old Ones came, many Palikúrs know
that when the moment of death comes, we will not
spend eternity on a barren rock set in an endless sea. We
know we will spend eternity with Jesus and with you, if
you have also been "lifted up by Jesus." Then we can
talk together and we will thank you for your prayers
and for sending the Old Ones to us. And together we
will praise our Lord for ever, and ever, and ever.

Until that day, I, Leon, leave you.

God, the Man
and Servo

BRAZIL

Chapter Four

In 1945 at age 15, the man—yet a boy in his native San Diego, California—had become a fugitive. A fugitive from most normal boyhood activities, his school work, and, worst of all, himself.

Albert Tompkins Graham lived in a strange twilight zone of self-conscious fear. His silent frustration with his deep inhibition had produced an "I couldn't care less" attitude toward school and most adult authority figures.

But God is tender, and his mind, mercy, and love past understanding. God has a plan for this frail unlikely boy, soon to become a man:

I have a job for you. I want you, and the helpmate I have chosen for you, to introduce my Son and take my words to a special people. They live in Brazil in isolation. They are sad and as lonely as you. You are now fragile and weak, but you will learn as most of my true servants learn that my strength is made perfect in weakness.

You will not have much of what you would call wealth. I know the less you will have, the more you will depend on me. Nor will the path I have chosen for you, your lovely helpmate, and children be easy. There will be sickness, thorns, hardships, bewilderments. You'll want to quit, but you won't. You will persevere and see sorrow turn to laughter. And all the while you will have my gift to sustain you—the Holy Spirit, my

presence—and my smile as I see you confound those who said
you could not do it.

You will spend your days in valuing that which will never
rust, decay, or evaporate, and many will call you a prophet, a
holy man, an eccentric. How little they know of me and the
strength of my love in the hearts of my children.

All this I will give to you, Albert Tompkins Graham. And to
your wife-to-be, Sue. Yet while I hold out my hand to give you
this, you must choose to take it.

Through the witness and ministry of Scott Memorial
Church in San Diego, Al Graham did choose to reach
out to God. In his fifteenth year he cried out for help.
Al learned that God's Son, Jesus Christ, could save him
from himself and help him overcome his fear, frustration and self-consciousness.

At first Al felt guilty. "The only time I call on God is
when I need help." But then he began to understand
that God had sent his Son to help those who couldn't
help themselves, to heal those who were sick—not those
who were well.

Al's spiritual healing was so remarkable that the
school principal called in his parents for a special
conference. "I don't know what has happened to your
son, but Albert's attitude has had such a dramatic
change, we've taken him out of the special tutoring
class. His motivation to learn is remarkable. I wouldn't
be surprised to see him graduate as his class valedicto-
rian." He did!

Later in college, Al married Sue, a charming, petite
girl from his home town with an infectious smile and
together they prepared to become Bible translators.
And then it happened—the first of many bewildering
obstacles.

"Perhaps you should reconsider your original goal," said a letter from the Wycliffe Board. "Would you consider becoming house parents at our children's home in Sulphur Springs, Arkansas?" And because they were warm and open to God's leading, they said yes they would, but only for a year.

As house parents, Al and Sue, with their three children, Karen, Steve, and Timmy, filled an important niche. But they continued to believe God had called them to Brazil and they kept praying.

"Listen to this," said Sue one day as she opened the noon mail. "It's a letter from Florence and Granville Dougherty. They want our job."

In a style that was later to become legendary, Al sent back the following reply. "We're glad you're interested in children's work. If you do come, there will be no maid. You'll have to wash your own clothes. There will be twenty kids to care for, and you'll have to pay your own rent."

By return mail, Al and Sue received another legendary reply. "We're coming."

A year later in 1959, Dale Kietzman, Director of the Brazil Wycliffe Branch, met the Grahams for the first time as they disembarked in Rio de Janeiro. With a warm, optimistic smile, Dale placed affectionate arms around Al's and Sue's shoulders. "We're glad you're here," he said.

Later as they rode in a taxi to the Wycliffe headquarters, Dale turned to Al and said, "What do you want to do while you're here?"

"Reach a tribe for Christ," said Al simply.

And just as simply Dale said, "It shall be."

"But you haven't seen my records," said Al.

"We won't worry about the records," said Dale. "I know linguistics isn't your forte, but there is more to translation than just being able to brilliantly analyze an unwritten language. Interpersonal rapport, an ability to understand and appreciate a new culture, and sensitivity to people are equally important. You and Sue have all these qualities. And I believe these, plus your obvious love for the Lord, will carry you over the rough spots, technical as well as cultural."

"Sounds like you've found a spot for us."

"We have," said Dale. "There are actually three spots, but I would suggest the Sateré people. They speak a relatively easy language and we'll have Dr. Sara Gudchinsky help you with your phonemic statement. (Al and Sue were to learn, as do all translators, there is no such thing as an easy language. Sateré has twelve vowels and eleven consonants!)

"Where do they live?" asked Al.

"On the banks of two small rivers in the middle of the Amazon. As near as we can tell there are about 300 Sateré."

"In the middle of the Amazon jungle?" said Al.

"Right," said Dale. "You'll have a 'nice' three-week boat ride."

It was actually well over a month, and it wasn't all that nice. The boat was unlike anything the Grahams had ever seen.

From the city of Belém, a lusty port town at the mouth of the Amazon River in northeastern Brazil, the

Grahams traveled up the Amazon aboard a sun-bleached single-stack woodburning steamer. At night, as well as during the day, people aboard the overcrowded boat hung their sisal hammocks from any available post, making the deck look like a maze of runaway spider webs.

After almost two weeks of hot, tedious river travel they reached the port of Parintines, which was only halfway to the Sateré people.

They had yet to look forward to a forty-eight-hour launch ride across a huge lake that looked and acted more like an ocean. Then a three- or four-day canoe ride up a narrow swift-flowing river choked with fallen trees, low tree branches, and overhanging saw grass filled with spiders, ants, and wasps. The Grahams were to travel up and down this river more than sixty times before Wycliffe's air arm—JAARS (Jungle Aviation and Radio Service)—could cut this arduous three- to four-week river travel to five air hours.

However, on that first trip to the Sateré people in January, 1960, it took the Grahams more than a month to cover that last three- or four-day journey.

The Grahams' Brazilian canoeman and guide had brought them across the lake from Parintines and into the marshy backwater of the Amazon without incident. Then just as they were within three days of their final destination, a group of Sateré men in a small dugout canoe rounded a bend in the river.

It was difficult to know who was more surprised. The Grahams were the first Americans these Sateré men had ever seen. While the Grahams' response was mixed—

startled and pleased to be coming finally to the end of a long journey—the Brazilian canoeman was plainly frightened. Never before had he seen men like these— four muscular men wearing tattered basketball shorts, their naked torso and legs covered with black paint. They fingered bows and arrows and their excited voices punctuated the air with unintelligible words which flowed through teeth filed to sinister points. The Saterés filed both top and bottom teeth in order to distinguish friend from foe. The Grahams knew the Saterés were peaceful and tried to put their guide at ease.

"If you wish to return to Parintines, I will take you," said the canoeman. "If not, I must leave immediately." With gestures and their limited Portuguese Al and Sue tried to urge their guide to continue on upriver, but were unsuccessful. Almost before they knew what had happened, the guide had beached the canoe onto a sandbar, unloaded the Grahams' equipment and supplies, shook hands, told them he'd return for them in September, and left. It was the last the Grahams ever saw of him.

With the memory and experience of their jungle training still fresh in their minds, Al and Sue made the best of this unexpected event by setting up housekeeping in an abandoned rubber hunter's shack. Rather than curse the darkness of their disappointment, they lit a candle of friendship with a nearby Sateré family.

"This was," said Al later, "a most important happenstance. We spent a month with this family learning all we could about the Sateré language and culture. It was the Lord's way of easing us into what was to become for me a difficult adjustment to a hard, indifferent, self-centered people."

When Al and Sue finally secured a large canoe and paddlers to take them upriver to their final destination, they discovered just how indifferent the Saterés could be.

"All we had to give the men to eat was a mixture of canned meat and rice," said Al. "After two days of this, the paddlers refused to eat and decided not to row anymore until they had fresh meat."

At night when the leaden Brazilian sky dumped its load of cold, heavy rain, the paddlers crammed under the canoe canopy and left the Grahams outside. They once spent nine hours outside during one of these downpours.

The Grahams noticed the same indifference when they tried to learn Sateré names for various objects. When Al pointed to a paddle, butterfly, fruit, or tree, the men responded with a silly laugh, unintelligible sounds, or silence. Later when Al hired a Sateré man to help him learn more of the language, the man made a cruel game of deliberately confusing him by giving the wrong names and incorrect meanings to sentences.

There was, however, one man who seemed truly interested in helping the Grahams learn his language. When Al asked this man what a certain object was, the man would jut out his lower lip and repeat the word in clear, crisp Sateré. And when Al and Sue weren't asking questions, this same man would tap Al on the shoulder, jut his lip toward the object, and repeat the word.

"Looks like this man really wants to help us learn his language," said Sue.

"Yeah," said Al. "I think he'll make a great language helper."

"Better get his name," said Sue.

"My name," said the little man with a broad open smile, "is Servo."

Chapter Five

Like many people, the Saterés have developed a cool, effective poison to destroy those who live outside the status quo. Americans would call it irony or mockery. Whatever the name, the intent is always the same—promoting embarrassment.

Though non-violent, such cynical criticism becomes a devastating weapon. Intuitively, the user knows such syllogisms will crush the victim's ego. This damage is sometimes irreparable.

The chief of Servo's village knew this. He also knew he didn't want these Americans, with their three children, living in his village. It had been three months since they had arrived and he felt threatened by their presence.

As chief, it was his responsibility to decide which men would work in which fields, who would cook and take the food to the men, who would hunt, and who would clean the village. Since he was chief, people obeyed him. But since the Graham's arrival, life in his village was changing.

Take the matter of hygiene. For as long as any Sateré could remember, their pigs, dogs, chickens, and any other reasonably sized jungle pets (birds, monkeys, river otters) and domestic animals slept, defecated and ate indiscriminately in the same living area as the family. Al and Sue saw this and immediately understood why the people were continually sick with parasites and typhoid, and why, when a Sateré woman gave birth, her baby often died from tetanus. And when the Grahams saw the leaky-roofed, dilapidated Sateré huts and their hammocks strung over smoldering cooking fires for warmth, they knew why many died from pneumonia and tuberculosis.

To initiate a change out of this maelstrom of physical misery, Al decided to sell medicine only to those households who would build and use a latrine. The Saterés thought this a small price to pay for the miracle-producing pills and injections, and most families complied.

Sue, whose heart broke over the terrible unsanitary conditions young Sateré mothers endured when giving birth, enacted her own solution. For those who would use them, Sue made up a kit containing sterile gauze, razor blade, thread, a receiving blanket and a layette, all provided free, courtesy of the Mennonite Central Committee. As attractive as this was to most mothers, it took Sue more than five years before the women felt comfortable enough to adopt the kit as part of the normal birth procedure.

But for the moment, the chief and most of the men in the village tolerated such eccentricities. After all, the Americans did provide endless hours of amusement for the isolated village.

"Look how he struggles by himself to build his house."

"Yes, and what is funnier than to see him hurt himself with a machete. Any man who cannot use a machete deserves to be laughed at."

"Yes, yes, that is funny, but it is even funnier to give him a dirty word when he believes it to be the true name of something. And then to hear him repeating these words over and over trying to learn them!"

When Al took his jungle training in southern Mexico before going to Brazil, he learned to laugh with his Indian friends when they laughed at a mistake he made with their language. This he also did with his Sateré friends—at least most of the time. But one day when he was doing his best to learn at least one vowel in a seven-, eight-, or nine-vowel word and they laughed over every one of his mistakes, Al became angry—at the Saterés—and God.

To escape the reminder of his failures, he took his canoe upriver and poured out his heart in prayer.

"Lord, how can You love these people? They consistently make fun at the things I do. If I trip or fall, they laugh hysterically. If I hurt myself badly, they really howl. They never offer to help work on the house, nor do they offer to help me carry equipment up the long steep trail from the river.

"They lounge on our table and chairs and we have to almost push them off when we want to use them. They finger our clothes and belongings. What's more, they blow their noses into their hands and wipe it on our walls. Lord, how can You love such disgusting people?"

As Al sat on the riverbank and prayed, he suddenly realized God had spoken to him.

I love the Saterés in the same way I love you—unconditionally.
Don't you realize your sin? All sin is just as repulsive to me as
the Sateré culture is to you. Furthermore, Albert Tompkins
Graham, I can be generous without a reason.

From that moment Al's feeling of disgust and hate
began to turn into a deep, caring love. It was a reflection
of the divine love that would one day turn the entire
Sateré village from darkness to light.

Soon it became apparent to the chief and villagers
that the man called Servo was beginning to clue Al in on
their pranks, and he, rather than Al, received the brunt
of their jokes.

"Oh, look," said the chief to his wife one day as Servo
walked past his house. "Look at that porcupine! Doesn't
he have a long nose? What does he do with it?"

"I suppose he just picks it," said the chief's wife.

On another day, the chief decided to punish Servo by
publicly exposing what he considered antisocial behav-
ior. As Servo made his way down the switchback trail
that led from the Graham's hilltop house to the pre-
ferred bottom land by the river, he noticed the chief
talking with a cluster of men and women from the
village. As he came within earshot, he heard the chief's
voice rise.

"What kind of man is it who sits all day and teaches
our language to foreign white people? Such a man is not
a man. He is a parrot—a parrot who sits when he should
work. Such a man is bad for our village. He insults the
spirits of the fields who demand we work together. Such
a man is bad for his family. If he only talks, how can he

work in his fields? And if he doesn't work, how can he provide food?

"I say such a man—or such a parrot—should, like the white people he teaches, leave our village and go to some other place on the river."

Servo knew what was happening, but walked past without a word. He felt embarrassment and shame because he had lost the approval of his peers, yet he resolved to work harder in his fields and not give in to public pressure.

There was something about the Grahams and what they were trying to tell him that made sense. "I do not understand why I like these white people," said Servo to his wife. "I don't understand what their words mean. Yet I feel what they talk about will be important in the future."

"Future?" said Servo's wife.

"Yes. In the long days to come when I know more about them and they of me, I believe, for a reason I cannot yet explain, they will be good for us and our village."

"Hmmm," said Servo's wife, "the only good reason for these white people being here in our village is that they give us medicine. Perhaps they will be like the man who was here before they came, the one who wore hair on his face. He said he had come to learn about us and when we gave him oranges, he gave us a hammock or a shirt. Why have you not asked for anything from these foreigners? You *are* a parrot, unable to talk, just as the chief says you are."

And so it went. For ten long, hard years, Al, Sue, their children, and Servo, together, and in their separate worlds, tried to make sense out of what was to be, from their points of view, a series of unexpected crises and adversities.

For the Grahams, one of the first serious crises occurred shortly after they returned to the Saterés for the second time.

"Your passports are in order," said the health officer in Belém, "but I am sorry you and your family cannot go into the interior. None of you have been vaccinated against yellow fever."

"What are we going to do?" said Al. "We've paid our passage and our luggage is aboard the ship which is about to leave for Parintines."

"Very well," said the health officer. "Under the circumstances, I will vaccinate you myself. Come with me to my office."

The Grahams quickly followed the health officer into a small cluttered storefront office at the end of a heavy wooden pier. While the health officer prepared the vaccine, he made idle chatter about not understanding why civilized people with intelligence would voluntarily live among "savage" Indians in the middle of the Amazon.

With his limited Portuguese, Al tried to explain that though the Saterés lived in isolation, they, like him, had souls. In God's sight they were equally as important as Brazilians or Americans. "I want to share this good news with these people," said Al.

Al could see the health officer wince under his words.

He didn't know if it was his poor Portuguese or the new concept that Indians were people, important to God.

"I don't believe Indians want your beliefs," said the health officer. "They are happy just the way they live. Next time when you come we will talk more. Now, give me your arm."

Timmy was first. After the health officer held the needle over the flame of a bunsen burner, Karen, Stephen, Sue and Al were vaccinated with the same needle.

Four weeks later, settled after their long journey, Karen, Stephen, Al, and finally Sue, succumbed to the flu-like symptoms of infectious hepatitis. For reasons unknown, nine-year-old Timmy was exempt. And for almost a month it was he who cared for his older brother and sister, and mother and father.*

Since the Brazilian government forbade foreigners to own and operate two-way radios, there was no way for the Grahams to contact Belém for help. The only alternative was to lay, day after day, in their hammocks praying and hoping the disease would burn itself out. It did for the children, but not for Al and Sue.

For a while, Timmy enjoyed his reverse role. But as the days crept by and he found less and less food to prepare, the novelty wore thin. By the end of the second week, the novelty was gone.

While he didn't fully understand the seriousness of his parents' sickness, he became increasingly aware of his mother's worsening condition. Each day small

---

*For further details, see "How Old is Nine" in Hugh Steven, *Night of the Long Knives* (Glendale, Ca.: Regal, 1972).

groups of Sateré women came, like Job's comforters, to visit and talk to Sue.

"Look how yellow she is today."

"I had a grandmother who looked like this and she died."

"True, true. Whenever a person's eyes look like this, he always dies."

"See how she vomits. That is a sure sign."

And all Al could do was shuffle along like an old man and weep whenever he thought of how much his wife and children were suffering.

By about the end of the third week, when Al felt all was lost, he called in his three children and explained, as best he could, that he and their mother were going to die. The children were to gather a briefcase of papers and take the boat downriver to civilization.

In later years, Karen, who grew into the same charming petite likeness of her mother, told how she felt about that moment.

> Stephen and I, like Mom and Dad, were sick with hepatitis, but we seemed to get over it in a couple of weeks. When I saw Mom lying there so still and sick-looking, I was scared, but didn't worry too much about it until Daddy called us in and said they were going to die and we were to get ready to leave.
>
> I was only eleven years old but I'll never forget that moment. The hut smelled and was almost too small for all of us. When the meaning of what my father said sunk into my mind, I could no longer stand to be inside with them. I ran outdoors, collapsed, sobbing at the foot of a tree, and began to pray.
>
> "Lord," I said, "if you will keep my parents from dying, I'll serve you full-time." Almost before I had finished praying, one of my little Sateré Indian friends came running up the trail all excited, yelling that two men, white like me, were coming up the river.

At first I didn't believe her, but when she insisted that it was true, Timmy and I ran down to the bank. Sure enough, there came Arlo Heinrichs and Dave Fortune (members of Wycliffe's Brazil branch). They were as surprised as we were when they saw us standing on the river bank waiting for them.**

While Arlo and Dave knew they were in the general area of the Sateré village, they were not sure exactly where the Grahams lived. "If it hadn't been for Timmy and Karen standing on the river bank," said Arlo later, "we might have missed the village."

While conducting a linguistic and language survey among other ethnic minorities of the Amazon, Arlo and Dave, at Director Dale Keitzman's suggestion, "dropped in" on the Grahams for a visit. It had been Arlo's hope, after a month without home cooking, to enjoy one of Sue's delicious meals. However, all thoughts of food vanished when the two men realized the seriousness of Sue's condition. Quickly they took command, made a stretcher for Sue, and began to close up the hut. Al, who felt morally revived with the visit of the two men, suggested they stay a little longer.

"Just leave everything to us," said Dave. "We're *all* leaving here in the morning."

For two days and nights Arlo and Dave paddled their sixteen-foot canoe carrying their sick passengers down-river to the vast lake.

Once on the lake, high winds began to whip the water into a sea of white caps. Skillfully maneuvering their canoe around the shoreline, Arlo and Dave reached the small outpost village of Ponto Alegre. Looking more

---

**Karen, now Mrs. Dan Everrett, related this incident in Mexico City on her way to Wycliffe's Jungle Training Camp as she and her husband prepared themselves to become Bible translators.

like drowned rats than humans, the tiny resolute band found shelter in an old dance hall just as the storm seemed to reach its fullest fury.

Years later Al would say, "Our canoe certainly would have been swamped and all of us drowned if we hadn't reached Ponto Alegre when we did. Never before or since have I experienced a storm with such force."

While Dave and Arlo welcomed a short respite from the hard non-stop rowing, they were deeply troubled and frustrated with the delay. No one spoke of it, but both men knew that unless they reached medical help fast, Sue would die.

"We need a motor launch to get us to Parintines," said Dave.

"There's one that comes into Ponto once or twice a month," said Al, "but who knows when that will be."

It was that night. Hardly believing their ears, Arlo and Dave looked at each other in disbelief when they heard the faint rumble of the launch's motor.

There is always a certain river captain stereotype—faded blue peeked cap resting at a rakish angle, dirty neck scarf, a three-day stubble beard, and a striped tee shirt hiding a heart of gold. This captain fit the caricature, except that his shirt hid not a heart of gold, but the heart of an opportunist. His price for taking them to Parintines was outrageously high.

"The Catalina plane will not land here today," said the young man at Parintines' dockside reservation office. "Two weeks ago some boys shot a sky rocket through the wing and the pilot is mad. If you wish to get aboard a flight to Belém, you will have to go fifteen miles downriver to the Romas Canal. The Catalina will land there but I cannot guarantee there will be room to take all of you. I hope there will be, as the next plane will not come for five days.

Though thoroughly exhausted, Arlo and Dave rowed the extra fifteen miles.

"I have room for four," said the pilot when he saw the canoeload of people.

"There are five of us," said Arlo, "and we must get to Belém immediately."

"Well, we'll try to squeeze you in," said the pilot, "but the lady will have to lay on the floor."

"I do not pretend to understand why you would take your lovely wife and children to live in such an uncivilized place as the interior" said the doctor in Belém as he talked with Al after treating Sue. "In my opinion, anyone who would do such a thing is a fool. We gave your wife twenty-one pints of glucose to combat her dehydration. Also, do you know she weighs only 98 pounds? If you had been delayed one more day she would have died! Under no circumstances must you ever take such a frail woman back to such an unholy place!"

Al smiled. He wanted to say something about checking with God on this matter, but said nothing. He was still weak from the long trip and the effects of hepatitis. As the doctor turned to leave, Al noticed the date on the wall calendar. It was April 4. "We'll go back before the end of the year," he said to himself.

And he did. Sue made a remarkable recovery and

they arrived back among the Saterés on July 4—three months to the day after the doctor's admonition not to return. It was, for Al and Sue, a moment of triumph. They felt elation over their victory and confidence that God was going to work among the Saterés. But, like Job's, their trials were just beginning.

Chapter Six

In 1967, seven years after Al and Sue had begun their work among the Sateré people, Al wrote the following words:

> After months of battling the effects of cerebral malaria (I sometimes acted as if I were spaced out on LSD), I began to wonder if God wanted me to give up the happiest work I had ever known. The malaria had left me so nervous and confused, I was unable to continue my Bible translation or linguistic program. I tried, but the work seemed beyond my capabilities.
>
> In my weakness, the Prince of Lies tried to teach me his half-truths. I began to say to myself, "What's the use? Let's give it up and go home. It doesn't work." The battle was almost more than I could stand and in my desperation I called out to the Lord for a sign—I put out a fleece. "Lord, if You want me to give up the Sateré work, show me. If You want me to stay, show me. Either way I am willing to do what You want." Within a week, we received a gift of $375.00 and a letter which said, "Al and Sue, this is to help you finish the book of Mark and to get it out to the Sateré people."
>
> Wow! What an answer! With this encouragement, believing it to be God's answer to us, Sue and I returned to our work. I was still exhausted and I could hardly work for more than a half-hour at a time, yet we pressed on, and on, and on, and the book of Mark was published.

There is a certain vulnerability among those who break spiritual ground and carry the seed of the Gospel into territory occupied by Satan. While the Prince of Darkness cannot destroy a child of God, he does, nonetheless, attack with insidious fury, especially when his territory is being contested.

The struggle between good and evil is always vicious and frequently subtle. Often only after the battle is over does the person who has gone through it understand that his struggle was not against human enemies, but against Satan and his evil armies.

Their first breakthrough came when Servo first believed and, like the Grahams, endured his own crises of growth. Their second came with the publication of the Gospel of Mark.

For Servo, his moment of truth occurred not in his village, but one afternoon when Al and he were translating at a workshop in the Belém Center.

"I must tell you, *Senhor* Alberto, you are using the wrong word."

"What word is wrong?" said Al.

"In all the nine times we have read and reread this story of how Jesus was crucified, I have not liked how you tell us that Jesus came back from the dead. I think it is wrong. You should say, 'He woke up.'"

"But Servo," said Al. "Jesus did come back from the dead. He didn't just wake up from a sleep. Jesus was dead. He was stiff. Every drop of blood was gone from his body. The soldiers put a spear into his side. He was dead, dead, dead!"

"It is impossible for a person who is truly dead to be brought back from the dead," said Servo.

"With God everything is possible," said Al. "God

raised his Son Jesus from the grave to show us he was stronger than death. He did it also to show those who truly believe and desire to follow and obey Jesus, that they no longer have to be afraid of dying."

"What of those who killed him?" said Servo. "When did he get his revenge?"

"Jesus did not seek revenge," said Al. "He forgave his enemies."

"If this is true," said Servo after a long thoughtful pause, "then I will follow him."

Servo's village was alive with excitement. No Sateré before Servo had traveled so far. Some had traveled to the government outposts on the river, some had even been to Parintines, but none had ever been to the big city of Belém and returned to tell about it.

Later, when the sun had lost its heavy heat and a breeze, cool and refreshing, rustled the bone-dry palm fronds on the roofs of the Sateré huts, Servo called everyone together. While the villagers hadn't understood his reasons for working closely with the Grahams, they had come to respect his honesty and hard work. It was rumored that when the old chief died, Servo would be named his successor.

Servo's three married sons came first and flopped themselves into limp, dirty-gray hammocks that hung from the smoke-blackened ridgepole of Servo's house. Their wives seated themselves on low footstools, crossed their ankles, and extended their bare legs into a common circle. The women, mostly in their mid-teens, watched their children as they tried to catch the tame chickens pecking at invisible insects on Servo's hard-packed dirt floor. And behind the members of the family stood the villagers, anxious for words and news of the big city.

After explaining about sky canoes and canoes with wheels that could carry more people than there were in their village, and about huts as tall as the highest trees, Servo began to tell them about a new treasure he had found.

"Most of you gathered here know how death took away my father when I was a young child. It was my grandmother who brought me to manhood. When I grew older I went from village to village looking for work to do in exchange for food to eat.

"While I wandered, I met Sabrina. I desired to help her and she desired my company. I asked her father for her, performed the ant dance, then took her into the jungle, and when we returned, she was my wife.

"Sabrina gave me three children, and then she died. I was very sad. Sad because I did not have a father and sad because I did not have a wife. I left my children in the care of others and again began to wander.

"One day I met a rubber hunter and he taught me to speak like the outsiders. This man also taught me to become a merchant and for a while I worked buying and selling things. During this time I married two more times. The wife I now have came to me a widow with children of her own.

"And then one day, when these white people came to live with us, I was asked to be an oarsman. When they first came, I could not understand why they had left their land to come to Brazil. But unlike some of you, I thought it good that they should want to live in our village.

"Many of you who once thought they were from the devil have changed your opinion. Look how many children we now have in our village. Since the midwives use the clean razor and thread, our newborn children no longer die. Most of you have learned to read and understand the paper that speaks our language. These have been good things for our village.

"Yet there is more. All the days of our lives we have believed the witch doctors when they have told us that our happiness comes from having more land, two wives, or from becoming drunk. But I have worked on the paper that comes from God and have learned that we have been deceived. I have called all of you here to my house to tell you that a light has come to our village.

"One day when I was a boy I was lost in the jungle. I tried to find my way back to the village but couldn't. I wandered into a swamp and there I spent a dark night, lonely and frightened. In the morning I walked toward the light of the rising sun, out of the swamp. And now, since I have decided to stick to the Words of Jesus Christ, I have seen a new light. It is like I am walking out of a dark, lonely swamp.

"Before, when *Senhor* Alberto and I worked to put the words Jesus said on paper, I would lie in my hammock at night and think about them. Is Jesus really the Son of God? Is he really going to come back to earth again? If he does come back, will I go through the great fire?

"Now I tell you, if you stick to Jesus' Words, you will

never go through the great fire. Many of you say among yourselves that his words are false. But I tell you, if you stick to Jesus' Words, a new light will come and he will teach you new things."

No one had moved or said a word during Servo's long, detailed story. But now they began to chatter. Some mocked, calling him a friend of the white man. When one person asked him what new things God had taught him, many laughed.

"God is teaching me that I must change my old way of thinking," said Servo. "God is telling me that I should not desire other people's land. He is teaching me I should leave off the ugly things that come out of my mind—things like killing for revenge, wanting two wives, or wanting someone else's woman.

"I have learned other things also. Before I stuck to Jesus' Words, I did not see the blue of the sky or the different greens of the trees when I walked through the jungle. When I saw a bird I thought only to kill and eat it. I did not think of them as beautiful.

"But now it is different. Now that I have come to know the Maker of all things, the different greens of the trees, the color of the flowers, and the beauty of the birds have become food for my eyes."

Most of the villagers who heard Servo's words that first evening left, warning him to abandon these new thoughts or the great anaconda would bring calamity upon his head and upon the village.

"You tell words that are new," said the villagers, "words we cannot believe. We know it is the thunder that speaks to the anaconda, and at night, when the witch doctors go to the river, they receive its message to us. We know it was out of the anaconda's womb that people, animals, and fish came, that from its body the rivers and seas flow, and from its dung the earth was made. It is the great anaconda we must worship, not this 'true' God and his Son you call Jesus."

Servo's three sons were the last to leave. As they did, each placed a hand on Servo's shoulder. "We do not fully understand all the things you have told us," they said, "but we all want, like you, to stick to the Words of Jesus."

Servo smiled. "I, like you, do not yet know all there is to know. We will learn together."

Chapter Seven

"If two or three of you who are named after me will get together after I am gone to talk with me, then I will come, too, and be there with you" (Matthew 18:20—Satere translation).

Like all true believers who enter into a vital, responding relationship with God through his Son Jesus, Servo was to learn that God works in ways different from man. He was to learn, as King David learned many years before him, that a good man does not escape all trouble, but that the Lord has promised to go through the trouble with the believer.

"What has happened to my son?" screamed Servo's wife when she saw Servo carrying the limp form of her eight-year-old son in his arms.

"His foot has received the fangs of the poisonous snake," said Servo.

"Ahhh!" screamed Servo's wife. "Do you see what happens when you stick to the Words of Jesus? My son will surely die. And you—you parrot—have made this happen!"

"I'm sorry, Servo, there is nothing I can do for your son," said Al later as he examined the boy's leg, swollen three times its normal size. "His coma is deep and I'm afraid the poison has reached his intestines."

"Is it not true, *Senhor* Alberto, that Jesus can cure people?" asked Servo.

"Yes, it is true as you say," said Al, "but sometimes—"

"Then," interrupted Servo, "let's ask Jesus to cure my son. If you say Jesus can do it, I believe he will."

Never before had Al's faith been put to such a test. Instinctively he wanted to point out that sometimes God uses trials, sickness, and even death to bring glory to himself.

Instead Al said, "Servo, the Scriptures say the believers should gather around, lay their hands on a sick person and pray for his healing."

Late that afternoon the villagers stood and watched in perplexed silence as Al and Servo—white man and Indian—knelt together, laid hands on the young, frail child's head and painful swollen leg, and asked God, in Jesus Name, to heal him.

"Isn't it wonderful that Jesus is going to cure my son?" said Servo as they finished praying.

"Yes," said Al weakly, "it is."

Al had prayed in faith, but the odds seemed overwhelming. "It will take a miracle," he said to himself.

Al was right. Anyone could see that the boy was dying, but the God who controls all nature and causes the lightning to flash from the clouds, performed a miracle. During the night, the high 90 degree jungle temperature suddenly fell to almost freezing. "We thought it was going to snow," said Al. "The low temperature was just what was needed to slow the body's absorption of the venom."

Although it was no surprise to Servo, Al and Sue marvelled when they saw the boy, several days later, alive and well, playing with his friends.

God had given Servo perfect faith to believe his son would be healed. Yet a few months later Servo almost lost his new-found faith over the failure of his crops.

"You know, *Senhor* Alberto, I broke Sateré custom when I planted my fields alone," said Servo one day as he and Al walked single file through the jungle.

"No Sateré ever works his fields alone," continued Servo, "but since I have stuck to the Words of Jesus, no one will help me. This year after I planted my field, it looked like my crops would be bigger than everyone's. I even told the men of the village that the God who healed my son was giving me good crops.

"But then God did not send the rain and my manioc died. Now I have no food. Why, *Senhor* Alberto, would God do this to one who sticks to his Words?"

The first thought that came to Al as he walked behind Servo was, "Servo, we don't always understand these things immediately, but later on God shows us the reasons." But just as Al started to speak, a strange phenomenon occurred. He opened his mouth and these words came out: "Servo, this is an illustration to you that the Word of God is going to die among your people if you don't plant it. I want you to plant it again and this time it's going to grow."

Al finished speaking and shook his head in disbelief. It was as if he had listened to himself speak on a tape recorder. Servo suddenly turned around and faced Al. "*Senhor* Alberto," he said in a surprised voice, "you didn't say those words!"

"What do you mean I didn't say them?" asked Al.

"You didn't say them," said Servo, "because they were spoken in perfect Sateré, without any accent."

Today Al and Sue know those were indeed words spoken by the Holy Spirit. But when it happened, neither Servo nor the Grahams fully understood its significance.

Frustration with language learning and Bible translation problems, the ordeal of river travel, and their never-ending battle with sickness and "calamities" continued. But through it all, Al and Sue became more and more aware of God's great love and care for them.

"At each point of crisis," said Sue, "we learned, in a new way, that the Lord wanted us to grow and trust him with our personal problems just as much as he wanted his Church established among the Saterés.

"This may sound strange, but he cared for us so much that the major spiritual changes among the Saterés occurred when we were out of the village. This kept Al and me from being infected with spiritual pride."

Sue was right. God showed them how much he cared for them by bringing Sue and Al home to San Diego in 1968 on a sick leave. Just before Al left, he gave Servo, another believer and four young men (non-believers) copies of the newly published Gospel of Mark.

In August, 1970, the Scott Memorial Church paid for

Al to return to Brazil so that Servo could help make corrections on the Gospel of John.

When he arrived in the village, Al learned that Servo's wife had recently died and that Servo was deeply distressed. Al told the people not to tell Servo that he had arrived, because he wanted to surprise him. And he did! Al walked to Servo's house and found him lying in his hammock. When Servo saw Al, he jumped to his feet, hugged Al, and began to cry.

"Oh, *Senhor* Alberto," said Servo, "I have been praying for the Lord to send you. And in his goodness, he has answered my prayers."

During his six-week visit, Al found that Servo, depressed and spiritually discouraged over the loss of his wife, soon regained his enthusiasm for life and for the Word. This was especially so when he discovered Al had come to work through the Gospel of John. Al was excited and encouraged when he discovered the Holy Spirit had used the Gospel of Mark to bring the four young Sateré men to faith in Christ. Furthermore, each of the men had, in turn, produced a brother in the Lord. Al also discovered a number of young men who had taught themselves to read because they wanted to be able to understand God's "Paper."

A year later, both Al and Sue returned to continue their Bible translation work among the Satterés. As the months and years passed, the Grahams' church and friends who had prayed and supported them for many years began to be singularly blessed with reports trickling out from that tiny dot in the Amazon jungle.

"A small church has been established in our village," wrote Sue. "Servo is now the pastor as well as the village chief. At first those who gathered at his house came out of curiosity. Now Servo, his new wife (a believer), his sons, and about thirty others gather eagerly each Sunday for Scripture reading and study.

"In the last three years several other new churches have been established, one upriver from us and two downriver. There are just a few believers in each of those villages, but interest in the things of the Lord is increasing."

And Al wrote of what he found after he returned to the Saterés.

"Sue and I had just arrived in the village—it took us six days to get here—when we heard singing. I knew I should go see what was happening, but was too tired.

"As the singing continued, I decided to take a look. I crept alongside the big longhouse the believers were using as a church, and looked around the corner. Just then the believers stopped singing and started to pray.

"When we left seven months ago, there was a real movement of the Spirit of God, but the prayer life among the believers was negligible. Now I couldn't believe my eyes or ears! There was Diu, who, when I left, wasn't even a believer, praying his heart out. And there was Celeste, who also hadn't been a believer, crying and praying. The sight touched me so much, I started to sob.

"For a moment I couldn't even catch my breath. I just leaned against the wall and slumped to the ground. I listened as everybody—children, grandmothers, grand-fathers—prayed real prayers from their hearts.

"As I sat with the tears slipping down my cheeks, I prayed. 'Thank You, Lord, for allowing Sue and me to plant your Word among the Sateré people. Thank You also for allowing it to take root and grow.'"

With the birth of the Sateré church, Al and Sue sensed a deepening burden to work harder on translation. They knew there could be no spiritual growth without daily feeding and instruction in the Word. But as they worked, the enormity of all that remained of the New Testament, the checking, revision, proofreading and printing sometimes polarized Al's translation energies.

Once when Al expressed his discouragement to Servo, Servo encouraged Al with a story. "*Senhor* Alberto, I once went to Black Earth City to tell the people about Jesus. Some of the people who ran away from our tribe asked me to come and tell them about the Paper from God. It was a city full of prostitutes and murderers.

"When I went there, I walked into the old church and saw the images they worshipped. When I saw this, I took all these things and threw them into the river. Then I preached from the Paper of God.

"Since then I have asked two brothers to go back to Black Earth City. Now each Sunday they stand and read the Scriptures in Portuguese and then in Sateré. No one has believed, but people are interested. They say they would like to have more of the Paper of God written in Sateré. I have told them that soon it will come."

With Servo's wise Solomon-like encouragement, Al had no alternative but to shake off the polarization and continue his long translation journey.

For a while Al made good progress, but then his translation program abruptly stopped. Graham's friends read about it in Sue's newsletter:

> During the last session in the village, we opened a successful school for the children. There has been renewed interest in learning to read, especially among the young ones.
>
> We also had to build a new house since ours burned down. At first we didn't understand why the Lord allowed this to happen. For the first time since coming to the village, we finally had an efficient house. Then one afternoon, the wind blew a piece of cardboard against a hot stovepipe, then onto the roof. The house burned to the ground.
>
> A woman standing by rushed in and saved a box which she thought was a hammock. But it was a box of precious language material. However, most of the Gospel of Luke was lost. We saved only this box and our two-way radio. Our hearts broke as we watched the house burn, especially after Al had worked so hard to build it. But we now praise the Lord for what happened.
>
> Since we had no place to live and since Al was having trouble with his eye, we decided this to be the best time to go to Belém for medical treatment. Al also had an ulcer behind his ear that would not heal. When we arrived in Belém, the doctors told us that these problems were more serious than we had thought. The ulcer behind Al's ear was a tumor caused by too much exposure to the sun. It would have to be removed. The doctors also said Al would have lost the sight of his eye if he had delayed treatment.
>
> We are thankful that the Lord, in his goodness, brought us out of the village when he did. We never would have left if the house had not burned. It shows us again how much he loves the Saterés and us.

While the Lord used the house burning to get the Grahams medical treatment, he also used it to strengthen the faith of the Grahams' older children, Karen and Tim. Before the birth of the Sateré church both had left the village to attend boarding school. Later they returned to visit their parents in their new aluminum house.

"There is little doubt in my mind," said Tim, "that in spite of all the storm, trials, and sickness, God is at work among these people. I would not have believed the change in the village had I not seen it with my own eyes. Before it was a village without laughter. No one seemed to laugh or even play. But now there is an unusual feeling of happiness and goodwill here. Children laugh and play tag with Dad."

It was this same feeling of goodwill that impressed Karen. "There were no believers when I left to go to school. In fact, no one seemed at all interested in the Gospel. But as I hiked around the village, I couldn't believe my ears. Everywhere I went little kids were singing and humming hymns. And at night when I walked through the village, I heard fathers in household after household reading the Scriptures and praying with their children.

"When I saw the deep friendliness and care shown by gifts of fruit and meat brought to my parents, and the people's desire to learn of the Lord, I wept. I wept remembering how hard it was during the first days when my parents were so sick and no one would help us.

"And I wept because all at once the fear and pain I felt when left at our children's home while Mom and Dad went back to the village, all seemed unimportant. In all probability, these beautiful people would not have had the Word if it hadn't been for my parents' obedience to what they felt the Lord wanted them to do.

"Whatever sacrifices I thought we had made were swept away when I heard a woman tell why she was glad my parents had come to live among them."

"Before they came, we all lived in darkness. We knew nothing of God. We lived by doing evil to one another. There was no happiness. We gossiped and cheated and were always afraid of the great spirit of the anaconda.

"Now we live in love, without fear. Most of all we live by the strength of God."

If We Perish,
We Perish

BRAZIL

Chapter Eight

The sun was warm, the breeze gentle, when I arrived at Wycliffe's Porto Velho center in north-western Brazil. But by mid-afternoon, as I walked along a red clay road with Eunice Burgess, a friend and colleague for more than twenty years, dark clouds began to obscure the sun and the wind grew crisp.

"It smells and feels like rain," I said.

"We usually get a little *drizzle* this time of year," said Eunice with an impish smile. "By the way the wind is blowing in those clouds, it looks like we'll just make it to the Sheldons."

Earlier, Eunice had casually mentioned that if I was looking for stories to illustrate God at work, I should by all means talk to Linda and Steve Sheldon. "They have a remarkable story," she said.

Eunice guided me to a neat bungalow with dark walnut-stained weather-worn slides and big screened windows as the first blinking lightning streaks heralded the ominous roll of thunder.

Once inside, Linda Sheldon, tiny, winsome, and full of life, offered us a frosty glass of iced tea. A few moments later her tall handsome husband joined us.

"Sorry to disturb your Sunday afternoon siesta," I said.

Steve smiled kindly, "I was just catching up on some overdue reading and correspondence," he said quietly as he extended his hand of welcome.

I felt very much at ease in this home. Linda's creativity was evidently displayed in her tastefully decorated home. And Steve looked like a professor of botany from an Eastern ivy league college. Here were two charming people giving their energies, personalities, and talent to provide God's Word for a tiny ethnic minority somewhere in the remote Amazon jungle. Both seemed serenely relaxed, as if nothing had ever disturbed their well-manicured lives. This illusion was shattered within ten minutes.

However, some of the picture I've described was not altogether wrong. I soon discovered Steve had taught political science at Northwestern College in Minneapolis. And while his field wasn't botany, his hobby was planting fruit trees and vegetable gardens—a hobby that endeared him to the Múra-Pirahã people with whom he and his wife work.

And I wasn't too far off base with my assessment of Linda. Her bright-eyed pert wholesomeness was cultivated in a small farm community in Iowa. And true to storybook virtues of America's Midwestern farm communities. Linda's hobby was homemaking and entertaining. (She had directed us to her big kitchen table and served the iced tea.)

"She's happiest when she's entertaining or sharing with others," volunteered Steve. "Village life has been hard on Linda for that reason. The Pirahã women, for reasons we haven't been able to discover, almost never talk to outsiders."

As I continued to sip my cool, refreshing drink, I looked around the room and noticed Psalm 112:7 neatly written out on a small decorative kitchen blackboard.

> "He does not fear bad news nor dread of what may happen, for he has settled in his mind that God will take care of him."

"That's a beautiful verse," I said. "Is it particularly meaningful to you?"

"We're just learning it as a family," said Steve. Then I saw Steve give his attractive wife one of those "shall we tell them" looks.

"Yes," said Steve, "this verse, especially the last part, and others like it, has a great deal of meaning for all of us. However, it took us a while to fully learn to appreciate its truth."

"Would you like to tell me about it?" I asked.

As Steve and Linda began to share their lives, I learned Linda had spent one summer in Canada with the Marine Medical Mission working with British Columbia's coastal Indians.

"It was a beautiful, exciting experience," said Linda. "But what impressed me most was meeting people who had never even heard of Jesus Christ. They knew nothing about his redeeming love.

"It was during that summer the Lord impressed me that I should become involved with Wycliffe. I just felt I wanted to work with an organization that spent its energies giving God's Word to peoples who had never heard. But I had a big problem—Steve."

In a few short sentences I quickly learned that while Linda's physical stature was diminutive, her faith and trust were not.

"Steve and I were already engaged," continued Linda, "and he had never talked about doing anything but teaching. Since the Lord had arranged this marriage prior to my feelings about going to the mission field as a Bible translator, I decided to trust him to work out the details. I told the Lord if he wanted me on the field, he'd have to do some persuasive talking to Steve."

In the fall, Linda returned to college and, true to her commitment, was silent about the new stirring going on inside her mind and heart. Yet she wondered how long she could hold out. It was shorter than she expected.

Several weeks after school had started Steve said, "You know, Linda, after hearing that Wycliffe speaker at the missionary conference last week, Bible translation sounds like interesting work. (Steve was also acquainted with Wycliffe work through his parents' support of a Wycliffe family.) Why don't we think about doing something like that? Would you ever think of becoming a Bible translator?"

Linda, hardly able to contain her happiness, said, "I've already thought about it!"

With their faith sparked by a desire to serve and a willingness to risk, Steve and Linda married, took their linguistic training, liked it, and asked for an assignment to Brazil. There were the usual adjustments to an overseas assignment—language study, learning the new culture, sampling strange foods, stomach upset, meeting new people, and feeling the indefinable excitement of being close to history in the making. Then came the first of two major tests.

Accompanied by Arlo Heinrichs, former translator to the Pirahã people, the Sheldons spent ten long, hot days aboard a cramped jungle riverboat before reaching their destination. Arlo spent a week introducing the Sheldons to the Pirahã people, helping them get settled in their new hut and pointing out interesting facts about the language.

"When you see a Pirahã stick out his tongue and touch his chin," said Arlo, "he's not making a rude gesture. That's merely their way of forming the letter 'L.' Also, since the language is tonal, the men use this to their advantage when hunting. They've developed a neat whistling system. The fluctuating pitch of the whistling allows the men to communicate with each other without disturbing the animals."

Arlo went on to explain that Pirahã women have a distinct langauge all their own. "You'll discover," he said, "they form their words way back in the throat."

At best, it's always hard to say good-bye to good friends. But, for the Sheldons, saying good-bye to Arlo was like suddenly being marooned on a desert island. This was especially true for Linda. Almost immediately after Arlo left, Steve came down with malaria.

Just to say "malaria" conjures up a Hollywood version of a teeth-chattering victim with a blanket pulled tight around his neck, heavy beads of perspiration standing out on his forehead like water on a newly waxed car. And this version is right. But there's more.

Steve's cerebral malaria gave him, in addition to

alternating high fever and chills, terrible back pain, headaches and delirium. For days, Linda watched her husband battle this nightmarish sickness. While fearing for her husband's life, she battled her own nightmare.

"After Arlo left," said Linda, "I had a terrible feeling of frustrating loneliness. Dozens of Pirahã people poked through our baggage to see what we had brought. Often people so crowded the room, I couldn't get to Steve. I couldn't even tell them to leave. I didn't know how. In fact, I didn't know how to speak to any of the people. Steve was too sick to talk or to respond to my chatter and I couldn't communicate with my six-week-old baby. I felt utterly alone."

This startling thought crushed Linda and she began to wonder to whom she could turn. In her desperation she went outside the village and took a long walk down a quiet jungle path. "I can't cope with this impossible situation," she thought. "I can't! I can't!"

But as she walked and thought about how the Lord had brought them to this place and what he had done for them in the past, a beautiful peace filled her. "I can't really explain what happened," said Linda. "The situation hadn't changed, but I just knew the Lord was going to help me get through. And when I walked back into the house, I no longer felt frightened or lonely."

It took Steve three weeks to fight off the debilitating flu-like symptoms of his first bout with malaria. But it would take him seven painful years before he went longer than several months without an attack.

"I just kept having one malaria attack after another," said Steve. "At one point I would just get over one attack and two weeks later I'd be down with another. Finally, Arlo, who was now director of the Brazil branch, said we would have to give up village living and go for a medical checkup."

While the directorate and others felt the best course of action was for the Sheldons to leave the Pirahã work, Steve and Linda felt otherwise. "In spite of all my malaria attacks," said Steve, "I never once felt we should leave. I suppose it never occurred to us that we had another option. We had committed ourselves to a translation and wanted to see it through."

The Sheldons communicated this desire to Arlo and said they would only consider giving up the translation if, after a medical examination, the doctor told them they must not return.

"Yes, I'm afraid you do have malaria," said the doctor to Steve after he had examined him.

Steve smiled. "I know I have malaria," he said patiently. "My question is, do you think I could return to the Pirahã area?"

"I know that river system," said the doctor. "It's one of the worst in all Brazil for malaria. And if you go back, I do not have any medicine I could give you that would prevent another attack. But as to whether you should return, I cannot say. I'm afraid you must make that decision."

"It's already been made," answered Steve, feeling that the Lord still wanted them to continue working in the Pirahã area. But as the months passed and Arlo received reports that Steve was sick again, Arlo wondered if he shouldn't have exercised his authority.

"After Linda and I returned to the village," said Steve, "the inevitable happened. Only this time it seemed my attacks were more violent than before—besides the delirium, I began vomiting until I thought there was nothing more to give."

As the reports of Steve's worsening malaria attacks reached Wycliffe's Brazil centers, the membership held a special prayer meeting for Steve's healing.

"I heard about this and was thankful," said Steve. "They had been praying right along, but this meeting somehow seemed different. I know that God touched me that night. That was two years ago and I haven't had a recurring attack!"

As I sat twirling the splinters of melted ice cubes in the bottom of my empty glass, Linda jumped up and promptly gave me a refill.

"You know," she said, "the Lord taught me a great lesson through that last experience."

"What was that?" I asked.

"When Steve was getting his medical checkup in Brasilia," said Linda, "I stayed here at the Porto Velho center. As I waited, prayed, and wondered if we should go back to the village, the Lord led me to Esther 4:16 where Esther says, 'If I perish, I perish.'

"As I read these words, I realized Esther had complete faith and confidence. She knew she would see results. And I thought the Lord was teaching me that Steve was going to come back healed from his malaria. Steve's doctor was from India and had spent several years doing extensive research, and I just felt sure he would give Steve some marvelous new medicine to cure his malaria.

"When Steve came back and told me the doctor hadn't done anything for him, that passage immediately came back into my mind. I realized I had incorrectly interpreted God's message. 'Okay, God,' I said. 'If we perish, we perish. If Esther can do it, so can we!'

"And just look what has happened! We didn't perish! God healed Steve with the marvelous medicine of prayer. What's more, he has given us a key man to help in the translation—Kaipagihi—a Pirahã man who has responded to Christ's personal love for him."

"That's a beautiful story," I said, "but I understand there's more. Didn't you have a rather emotionally charged experience with your son not too long ago?"

"In 1974," said Linda. "But that's another long story. Better have another glass of iced tea."

Chapter Nine

Finally it all came together—the wind and the rain and the thunder and the lightning—like the swelling crescendo of a great organ toccata. And for a while it seemed the afternoon storm emptied itself directly over the Sheldon's house. It was a fitting prelude to the story Steve and Linda were about to tell.

After living three months in Brasilia working as the Branch's acting director, Steve moved his family back to the village. There they again set up their translation work among the Pirahã people. They had only been back a few days when Nate, their eight-year-old boy, started to complain of his fingers and toes hurting at night. Steve and Linda examined him, but couldn't find anything wrong.

Shortly, Nate began to complain about pain not only at night but during the day. Then the Sheldons began noticing the tips of his fingers and toes turning chalk-white. It always seemed more pronounced when he had been swimming in the river and was cold. Finally the chalk-white fingers began to turn black and the discoloration started to spread down his fingers.

At this point, Linda radioed the Porto Velho center for medical advice describing Nate's symptoms. She was told to bring Nate in immediately.

"I'm afraid this is serious," said the doctor after he had examined Nate. "You must get your son to a hospital in Rio immediately."

"Immediately?" questioned Linda. "I don't want to go south alone and my husband is in the interior with our two other children. If the weather is bad, it might take a day or two for him to meet me here."

"My dear lady," said the doctor, "you must leave for Rio tomorrow morning. A delay of a day or two might result in the loss of your son's fingers, or worse, his life! It just so happens a colleague of mine is attending a medical conference in Rio at this very hour. I'll call ahead and have him arrange for someone to meet you at the airport."

It would only take two hours to reach Steve in the JAARS' single-engine Cessna. But if the pilot were to pick up Steve and the children and get back for the 10:30 flight to Rio, it meant starting out at 6 A.M.

"The problem is not the early flight," said the pilot to Linda. "It's the fog. There's always a low ground fog this time of year. Can't usually get off the ground much before 9 A.M."

It was Steve's custom to tune in his two-way radio each morning at seven to check with the Porto Velho center and listen for news of his colleagues. As he checked in that morning, he could hardly believe the words crackling out from the little box. "The dawn is clear and bright here at the center ... plane is already in the air ... close up house ... be ready to fly back within the hour."

No matter how organized or helpful a man is around the house, most are unable to execute the subtleties of selecting children's clothes and packing up a house without the punctilious aid of their wives.

"I just started going around in circles," said Steve. "I went into one room and started to do something and thought, 'Oh, I don't know what to do here,' and left it for another room. But somehow I did in forty minutes what usually takes Linda and me two days. We made the 10:30 flight to Rio!"

In a moment of crisis, the advertised soft splendor and spectacular setting of a Rio de Janeiro changes into a hard, bleak, nerve-jarring megalopolis. But most of the empty, hopeless, impersonal feeling of a big city without friends was eased by the doctor in Porto Velho who had arranged for his colleague to meet the Sheldons at the Rio airport.

"Mr. and Mrs. Sheldon, with all the hospitals and doctors in Rio, I would say you are unusually lucky to have been directed to me. I am only one of two or three doctors in all Brazil who has ever treated your son's disease." The doctor diagnosed Nate's problem as *arteritis*, a rare circulatory disease that destroys arteries as it moves through the blood stream.

Steve's and Linda's spirits jumped when the doctor told them of his experience and qualifications. But they plummeted after he had given Nate a thorough examination and said, "Although I have treated arteritis before, the only way to really give relief is to find out what's causing the problem. There could be a number of explanations."

"Can't you test for this?" asked Steve.

"We can, and under normal circumstances we would,"

said the doctor, "but here in Rio the laboratories are scattered all over town. It would take too long to make appointments, do the testing, and collect the results. I fear it's too late for this."

"I don't understand," said Linda. "What do you mean 'too late'?"

"The disease has advanced too far," said the doctor. "Gangrene has set in. If your child doesn't get immediate treatment, he will die."

All during the interview, eight-year-old Nate sat, listening, gripping his right wrist with his left hand in an effort to stop the pain in his fingers. The doctor had assumed the Sheldons were from the United States Embassy and that Nate would not understand Portuguese. But prompted by second thoughts, the doctor suddenly turned to Linda and said, "Nate doesn't understand Portuguese, does he?"

"Yes," said Linda weakly, "he does."

At that point the doctor asked Linda to take Nate out of the room. He then turned to Steve and said, "I know they are studying this disease at the National Institute of Health in Washington, D.C. They have all the laboratory facilities there and perhaps could come up with something immediate that would stop the spread of the disease."

"We'd rather not go unless it's absolutely necessary," said Steve. "Can't you do something here?"

"I am sorry," said the doctor. "The only thing I can do is to start him on cortisone, but you still must get him to an equipped hospital for testing."

The Sheldons left Rio that very afternoon—Linda

and the children to Porto Velho to pack, and Steve to Brasilia to arrange for their exit papers. Steve also called his parents and asked them to make arrangements at the Washington hospital.

"I was numb with the shock of the news and the dread of all we had to do before we left the country," said Linda, "and in the confusion forgot about the impact all this was having on poor Nate. I knew he was in pain and I knew he had understood what the doctor had told us. But as we bumped along in the bus to the airport, I noticed Nate sitting back, singing a Portuguese chorus, 'I will praise, I will praise him, he's my Savior.' I wept.

"While he never verbalized it, I felt that Nate had perfect confidence in the Lord. He had seen the Lord do some miraculous things in the village and I believe he felt the Lord would do the same for him."

While the Sheldons waited for their exit papers and plane tickets, and took care of the myriad of things one does before a major trip, they learned something about Washington's National Institute of Health.

There was a waiting list of several months and, since it was a research hospital, they would admit only patients who had a disease they were studying at the time. They also learned one had to be recommended by two doctors before he could be admitted.

With this news piled on top of everything else, the Sheldons were again distressed. But Steve's parents called with some encouraging news.

"You're not going to believe this," they said, "but when we called the hospital in Washington, we were able to talk with the doctor who is working on this very problem. He taught in Brazil and knows the doctor you saw there."

With hope renewed, Steve asked, "Did he say anything else?"

"Yes, the doctor said he'd take the Rio doctor's word that Nate has arteritis. That is, until they check it out. But if he doesn't have the disease, he'll be immediately discharged."

A month passed between the time Nate first complained of the pain in his hand and his arrival in the Washington hospital. He now limped and continually gripped his wrist in an effort to stop the terrible pain in his fingers.

The doctor assigned to the "Sheldon Case" greeted them, examined Nate and returned with his prognosis. "I'm afraid the doctor in Rio was right. And I'm afraid also we will have to amputate."

"You're not going to leave me here alone, are you, Mommy?" implored Nate as he walked with his mother and father down the corridor to his hospital room. "I'm scared of this big place."

Steve and Linda immediately realized their son was more concerned about the large, busy hospital than the possibility of losing his hand, and explained Nate's trauma to the doctor.

"Nate has spent most of his eight years living with about sixty Indians in the Amazon jungle," said Steve.

"I understand," said the doctor. "We'll arrange for you to stay with your son. One further detail I should mention. Until we isolate the cause of your son's illness, we are suspending all medication."

And so the tests began. Probes, x-rays, analyses of

urine and blood, conferences and consultations with covies of doctors.

"It's a good thing this is a government hospital and you're not paying all the bills," commented a doctor one day to Steve. "It would take you a lifetime to pay them off."

Steve and Linda were indeed thankful and happy they didn't have the expense of the testing. But they were more excited with Nate himself. At first he gradually kept declining. Then they noticed he cried less and less with the pain.

"Am I seeing things?" said Linda to Steve one day over coffee. "Did you notice that Nate's fingers aren't quite as dark as they were?"

"Yes," said Steve, "I've noticed. Let's ask the doctor about it."

"A disease this serious does not get better without medical aid," said the doctor when the Sheldons asked him. "And I must also warn you not to say anything to Nate. We will still have to amputate as soon as he's adjusted to the trauma of the hospital."

The doctor so intimidated the Sheldons they had no alternative but to return to their previous vigil of prayer and waiting. Yet they could not dismiss what they saw happening. And then what had been apparent to Steve and Linda became apparent, albeit reluctantly, to the doctors.

"I don't want you to become unduly excited," said the doctor one morning to the Sheldons. "We are going to delay the amputation. Our tests seem to show that Nate's blood is normalizing. You know, of course, that we've done a complete blood exchange, but we think some mistake has been made in the lab. We'll have to do more testing."

As the days passed and the tests still proved inconclusive, the blackness in Nate's fingers became whiter and whiter until the doctor finally conceded, "The disease itself appears to be gone, but the gangrene is still present."

But with the passage of still more days, the Sheldons and the doctors saw a miracle take place. Nate's fingers and toes became whiter and whiter until the discoloration showed only in his fingertips. For a while they looked like burnt marshmallows. Finally, when the black scabs peeled off, all that remained for Nate to show people was a tiny white, flat spot on each of his fingertips.

It took five weeks of testing and close observation, plus three months of weekly visits before the doctors pronounced Nate cured.

"As we look back now," said Linda, "we see clearly how the Lord guided and was with us during those darkest moments. I don't want to give pat or simplistic answers as to why God allows suffering. But I believe in our case the Lord called us home from Brazil for a specific purpose."

Steve and Linda both agree they will probably never know all the reasons, but they do know there were several people who came to know the Lord as a direct result of the miracle the Lord performed in Nate's life.

One of these was a doctor who told Steve he was not too serious about his "religious" life. After Steve shared how God had worked in Nate's life and in the details of getting them to Washington, the doctor made an appointment to see his pastor. "I've been impressed this week with the way God has worked in the lives of a young family," he said. "I feel it's about time I began to think seriously about trusting the Lord. Can you help me?"

As the Sheldons shared their story in churches and informal gatherings, they found a new avenue of ministry opening to them. "Instead of asking us about the length of the snakes around our jungle home," said Steve, "we found people sharing the deep concerns of their lives—problems with their teenagers and marriages."

One of the stories people liked to hear was the way the Lord provided housing for the Sheldons during their stay in Washington. When Steve's parents, who live in Colorado Springs, learned that Steve and Linda would be staying in Washington during Nate's recovery, they asked their church to pray for their needs. A member of that church phoned one of his friends in Washington and asked him to meet the Sheldons at the airport. He did and took them into his home for several days, but it was small and they knew they shouldn't stay too long. Just as they were wondering where they could find a place of their own, they were offered an apartment vacated by a military man away on business.

A few weeks later when the man was due to return, they knew they would have to find other housing, but where?

A short-haired, no-nonsense-looking woman who could have been a sergeant in the Marines gave them the answer. She knocked on their door and asked, "Mr. Sheldon?"

"Yes."

"I'm Pansy Baker. I'm here to find you a place to live."

And she did! In a couple of days she found a house that had been vacated by a couple who had gone to Florida for the winter.

"How did you find out about us?" asked Steve.

"You have friends in Billings, Montana," said Pansy. "They heard about Nate and wrote to their parents in Minnesota. They, in turn, presented your needs to their Sunday school class. A woman in the class said she had a friend in Washington. She called this friend and told her about your situation and asked if she'd mind taking you under her wing. I am that friend."

I set my glass on the table, picked up my notes, and turned to leave. "What about the doctor that treated Nate at the National Institute of Health?" I asked. "What was his reaction to Nate's recovery?"

"He has become a good friend," said Steve, "but as yet he will not admit it was God who healed Nate. During the days when Nate's condition was improving, he would just say, 'We can't understand it, but there is something there we are not finding.'"

I knew I had more than enough material for a story on the Sheldons, but I had one more question to ask. "Is there anything else you learned through this experience?"

"I think God allows these kinds of experiences in our lives," said Steve, "to teach us lessons of trust. For example, the Lord gave us a verse in John that was a great help: *You don't understand now what I am doing, but some day you will.* Also, others were taught and encouraged as they saw us go through this experience. Both Linda's parents and mine found they learned to trust the Lord in new ways."

"We sometimes wonder why the Lord picked us out," said Linda reflectively. "But we know that through these kinds of experiences, God gets the glory. For this reason Steve and I consider all we've been through a privilege!"

The rain had stopped when Eunice and I left the Sheldons. It had been a heavy rain, almost an inch in an hour. The breeze was once again gentle; birds chirped in nearby trees.

"I've been thinking," I said, "about a letter Joe Bayly sent to one of our young Wycliffe members whose wife died suddenly with a brain tumor. He wrote, 'God must love you very much to have entrusted you with such suffering.'"

"I believe the Sheldons must also feel much loved by God," said Eunice. "Did you notice they came through it without a tinge of bitterness?"

"Yes," I said. "I believe they've learned what the apostle Paul was talking about when he said that if we are to share Christ's glory, we must also share his suffering."

Light Obeyed
Increaseth
Light

BRAZIL

VENEZUELA

GUYANA

FRENCH
GUIANA

PALIKÚR

MAKUSÍ

SURINAM

KARIPÚNA

COLOMBIA

APALAI

OIAMPI

Rio Negro

MAKÚ

HIXKARYÁNA

MANAUS▲

SATERÉ

BELÉM

ASURINÍ

URUBÚ

SÃO LUIZ

MUNDURUKÚ

GUAJAJÁRA

CANELA

DENÍ

TÚMA

APURINÃ

JAMAMADÍ

MÚRA-PIRAHÃ

APINAYÉ

PAUMARÍ

PARINTINTÍN

KARITIÁNA

PORTO VELHO

KAYAPÓ

RIO BRANCO ●

RIKBAKTSA

PERU

SURUÍ

KARAJÁ

CINTA-LARGA

KAYABÍ

KAMAYURÁ

WAURÁ

MAMAINDÉ

NAMBIKUÁRA

PARECÍS

XAVÁNTE

BAKAIRÍ

CUIABÁ▲

BOLIVIA

BORÓRO

BRASÍLIA▲

SALVADOR

MAXAKALÍ

KADIWÉU

TERÊNA

BELO HORIZONTE ●

KAIWÁ

PARAGUAY

SÃO PAULO ●

RIO DE JANEIRO ●

GUARANÍ

KAINGÁNG

ARGENTINA

PORTO ALEGRE ●

URUGUAY

Chapter Ten

In Bona, the breeze that sweeps across the airstrip and down into the village where the Koehns live feels like a blast from the sun's open doors.

There are insects, too. Great hoards that nip and pick and sting and fly into your eyes and nose. And there are mosquitoes—the kind that carry malaria.

It's like this now, and it was like that in June, 1962, when Ed, Sally and their four-month-old daughter, Margaret, came to live among the 200 Apalaí people on the Paru River. With them on that June day was Pete Wiessenburger, a classic "Little John." It was Pete's job to introduce Ed and Sally Koehn (pronounced Cain) to the sturdy barrel-chested Apalaí people, help them with the language, and get settled in this, their first translation allocation.

From Belém it had taken them seven days aboard a wood-burning riverboat to reach the small port town of Almeirim. Once there, they chartered a Cessna from a rubber hunting company and flew to a remote jungle airstrip. From there they took a short 90-minute canoe ride into the Apalaí village where they would make their home.

It was hot indeed on that June day. But in their

youthful enthusiasm, Sally and Ed tried to shrug off both heat and insects. They had work to do and wanted all their energies concentrated on how they could best accomplish it. Their game plan was simple: learn the Apalaí language and customs, translate the New Testament into that language, be a good neighbor, and in their "spare time" introduce a program of community development.

Ed, with Pete's help, began building their first jungle hut. In the evening, he and Sally, with smudge pots under the table to drive away the mosquitoes, tried to memorize Apalaí words and phrases. They worked hard, until they were exhausted.

The long hours on his father's farm in Edmonton, Alberta, had engrained the traditional Judeo-Christian work ethic into Ed. It also gave him a love for mechanical work. In fact, it would take several years before Ed would feel comfortable with long sedentary hours behind a translation desk. He would always feel a tug to get his hands dirty—but it was to be a natural lead-in for the community development program he would begin among the Apalaí.

Sally, too, was in her natural element—or so she thought. Keeping house and experimenting with foods had always been a hobby for this young woman from Tennessee. Also, for as long as she could remember, "missionary," especially "pioneer missionary," had been a household work in her parents' home and her Christian community.

But as the hot, insect-filled days and nights wore on,

this attractive Southern woman with a wide warm smile and soft dark hair began to understand what it is like to live in a cross-culture community.

Before their actual arrival, Ed and Sally studied photos taken by the first survey team and spent many hours praying for God's Spirit to prepare the hearts of the Apalaí to receive God's Word. On Kodak photo paper, the Apalaí appear as they are in real life—colorful, handsome people. Both men, women and children wear their thick licorice-black hair in a Prince Valiant cut. Their skin has a sheen—a luster of copper mixed with orange. And except for a scarlet loincloth for the men and a small front apron for the women, the Apalaí work, hunt, eat, and sleep naked.

Ed and Sally's prayers, natural interests and presuppositions gave them a sense of love and concern for the Apalaí; intellectually Sally knew God loved them. Therefore she loved them. It was idealism at its best.

But then some things happened to shatter what Sally would later call her "worked-up love for the Apalaí." First, when the Koehns' food supplies were delayed they were forced to eat only native foods. But the Apalaí had barely enough for themselves. Why should they share with the outsiders?

Next came the inevitable—malaria. First Ed, then baby Margaret.

It's quiet in Bona. There are no cars, trucks or doors that slam. There are barking dogs, an occasional crowing rooster and people who chatter. The village is small, perhaps a dozen families, and, when the sun is high, activity stops. Even the dogs and chickens find little reason to wander.

There are, however, the insects—flies that buzz and beetles that shimmer in the waves of vibrating heat which seem to bounce off the hard ash-gray dirt.

Ed and his little daughter lay in their hammocks under a makeshift shelter, trying to fight a fever that matched the outdoor midday heat. Ed felt miserable and found some relief in complaining to his sympathetic wife and colleague. But Margaret only cried, whimpered and cried some more. All Sally could do was pray and wave away the flies and bugs. She felt the cold nauseating waves of fear grip her stomach as she sat physically helpless, waiting for the tide to turn.

The days passed and Ed improved, but six different types of malaria medicine plus antibiotics failed to arrest Margaret's sickness. After a month the Koehns decided to take their daughter out to Belém for medical attention.

But transportation posed an immediate problem. The rubber company's plane that could have flown them out was grounded—a gas shortage. This left the treacherous Para River as the Koehns' only exit route. And when a Brazilian rubber-hunting family passed by, Pete Wiessenburger took Sally and her sick fever-ridden baby down the rapid-infested river.

Ed stayed behind to start building rapport with the Apalaí. When Sally left, she promised to send word of their safety with the first boat coming back upriver. It was six weeks before Ed knew for certain his wife and child had made it to Belém.

The letter gave skimpy details and didn't mention what it was like to sit hour after hour in a cramped ungainly craft trying to bottle-feed Margaret through fever-blistered lips, change diapers, and shield her from burning sun and tropical rains. And it wasn't until later when Ed joined them that Sally told him how she felt about returning to the Apalaí. With every rapid she descended and every waterfall she walked around, Sally had repeated the same phrases over and over.

"I will not go back. They don't care for my baby. They don't care if I live or die. They didn't give us food. No one can raise children in a place like that. Who can live with all those bugs? It's impossible. I will not go back. We'll just have to find some other kind of work at Belém."

As she vigorously replayed the strong, negative feelings she had during the trip, Sally also shared new feelings that arose out of an extraordinary event.

When Sally arrived in Belém, she took Margaret directly to the hospital. There the doctor quickly diagnosed the ailment as cerebral malaria which caused no threat to her life. What a relief! When Margaret had not responded to the antibiotics and malaria medicine, she had been afraid of leukemia.

"However," said the doctor, "since your daughter's fever was so high and endured for so long, we cannot be sure there has not been brain damage."

Sally returned to the Belém center to anxiously pray and wait. Upon arrival, she found two letters waiting for her. One was from her mother in Tennessee, and the other from Ed's mother in Edmonton.

As Sally read them, she could not believe her eyes.

Both were written on the same date, both said they had felt a great burden for them, and both said they felt God urging them to pray for Margaret. As she compared the letters, she realized her two mothers had been praying during the time Margaret's fever was highest. In that moment Sally knew God was going to preserve Margaret's mental stability. And in later years, as Sally told the story, she would say, "And God did. There is absolutely no brain damage."

With prayer and skilled medical attention, Margaret quickly regained her health. And under the more relaxed and supportive conditions at Belém, Sally once again was forced to grapple with her feelings about the Apalaí. As she struggled, the words of a little poem by Torrey kept coming to her mind:

Light obeyed increaseth light,
Light rejected bringeth night.

Then she remembered a difficult time she once had during college and the words her mother had sent from Jeremiah 12:5:

If thou hast run with the footmen, and they have wearied thee
... then how wilt thou do in the swelling of Jordan?

As Sally allowed the Holy Spirit to work in her mind and heart with this and other Scriptures, the Lord revealed a new truth. She discovered that she would never make it if she went back dependent on her own contrived strength or with her false enthusiasm. Slowly it dawned—love is not a feeling, but an action. Sally began to understand that the Lord in his own way and time would love the Apalaí (and where they lived) through her. She claimed his promise to her and accepted her charge—to walk in obedience to the light he had given.

Ed and Sally obeyed that light—obscure at first. But as the months and years passed, their light of purpose and resolve grew steadily brighter—not necessarily easier, but brighter.

The problem of bugs that once seemed so impossible was solved when Ed explained their new house plans. The answer? He would enclose the rooms with mosquito netting. Later a JAARS plane made travel to Bona easier and safer. And a two-way radio gave them that extra sense of well-being and broke their complete isolation.

When a tribe first hears that the true God of the universe has communicated his desires and will in a Book, they are hesitant to accept an alternate spiritual lifestyle. There is first the struggle against Satan. This undisputed territory has been his since the beginning of time. And then there is the natural struggle common to all humanity—the resistance to change and to taking risks. Most find it a difficult struggle to grow out of the past and deal objectively with the present.

The Koehns knew this and were keenly sensitive to the natural reluctance of the Apalaí to cast off their centuries-old practices of animistic worship and witchcraft. Yet almost two years had passed since the Koehns first arrived and no one had outwardly indicated his desire for a spiritual change.

Soon after his arrival among the Apalaí, Ed felt he had discovered a key that would open an interest in the Gospel. He noticed their stark terror of death. Their animistic religious system gave them absolutely no hope

for life after death and Ed wondered when he would
have the opportunity to show them that, for the person
who truly has God's Spirit dwelling in him, death is no
terror.

That opportunity came one dark night with the awful
crashing of a tree.

Chapter 11

There are trees in Bona—tall trees that reach up two hundred feet into the sky. Trees with heavy branches festooned with clusters of leaves in every shade of green—olive and apple and shamrock and mint and more. Sometimes when the ground is soft after a heavy rain, trees fall over, such as the one that fell one dark night shortly after Sally and Ed had gone to bed.

It was a tree that Antonia, the 25-year-old wife of the village chief, had worried about for some time. She knew this particular tree was leaning more and more in the direction of her house.

In the two years the Koehns had lived among the Apalaí, no one had become closer to Sally than Antonia. She had accepted this outsider as her blood sister, and under her patient, cooperative and excellent tutelage, Sally had learned to twist her tongue around the difficult Apalaí words and sentences. In a word they were friends.

At first, all the Koehns heard was the creaking of wood, like someone trying to open a hard, rusted gate. Next came a kind of moan and groan, a shifting of weight—tons—, the slow crack-crack of splitting wood, and then the thudding crash of a colossus falling to earth.

Quickly lighting the Coleman lantern she had just extinguished, Sally grabbed her robe, slipped into a pair of Ed's shoes, and ran with Ed in the direction of the noise. To their horror they saw a huge pile of leaves and branches where Antonia's house once stood.

The icy sickening fear in Sally's stomach told her what her mind wouldn't—Antonia and her husband were dead. Instinctively she knew this, even though from under all the rubble she heard the terrifying screams of Antonia's four children calling out in the blackness.

While Ed ran back to their house for another lantern, machete and saw, Sally and another man searched for a way to reach the crying children. They found a small opening in the back and crawled through. While badly frightened and overcome with shock, the children were miraculously unhurt.

It was 9:30 P.M. when the tree fell. Forty-five minutes later, working with pole and lever, Ed reached Antonia's body. With tears in their eyes, Ed and Sally carried her limp form to an adjacent guest house. Tenderly, Sally, more from an unwillingness to accept death than from a hope of life, tried to restore Antonia's breathing. It was futile, of course, and Sally wept.

Though exhausted (it had taken until after midnight to reach Antonia's husband), Ed and Sally stayed to comfort and console Antonia's extended family. With tenderness Ed said, "Death comes to all, but those people who allow God's Spirit to live in their insides have a hope beyond this life. We have come to live among you because we believe God has sent us. He sent us here to share with you some wonderful news about his only Son. This Son is Jesus who has loved you beyond the strength of the greatest anaconda." And then they wept with those who wept.

Filled with remorse over the death of their friends, Ed and Sally returned to their house to catch a few hours sleep before dawn. As they slipped under the mosquito net, Sally remarked that while Ed had been telling the people about God's love and his promise of eternal life, she noticed the Apalaí seemed to pay serious attention to Ed's words for the first time.

"Perhaps," said Sally, "this is the beginning. In spite of our inability to fully explain God's love in their language, a seed was planted tonight."

Ed hoped it was true, because outside Antonia's oldest daughter had begun her death wail. The young girl wailed her plaintive question, "Where have you gone, Little Mother? I don't have a little mother. I don't have a little father. Where have you gone? Oh where have you gone?" over and over until her tear ducts ran dry and she fell into the dirt with exhaustion. She would, in despair, ask again and again, never expecting an answer.

But there was an answer. It came in 1972 with the publication of the Gospel of Mark. Then for the first time in their history, the Apalaí read for themselves about people who could be healed from sickness, about God's Kingdom, about Jesus who is strong—strong enough to hush a mighty storm and defeat Satan. And they read what one must do to become a follower of Jesus Christ. But most of all they learned about a death—Christ's death—about coming back from the dead—hope, heaven where God will wipe away all tears, and eternal life.

And when the Apalaí read and understood (they learned to read through Sally's literacy classes), many said, "God, I want You to help me. Teach me your Word so that I can be on it (obey it), so that I can be your follower."

But before all this happened, there was still the need for more seed planting, and another opportunity came just three weeks after the tree had fallen.

It happened after an all-night drinking festival. Community celebrations are common among the Apalaí. But week-long festivals occur only once every few years. There is seldom a formal announcement of such a festival. But all of a sudden great piles of manioc roots appear in front of the chief's house. These are peeled, grated and cooked into a special drink, then stored in dugout canoes to ferment. On this occasion, six canoes were filled.

Before the actual drinking and dancing begins, the young men of the village organize a traditional fish poisoning expedition. *Aisore*, a poisonous jungle vine, is gathered and clubbed into pulp. At daybreak, the men find a quiet river channel, release the poison by stirring the *aisore* into the water, and in a short time the milky-white substance flows down the channel. The young men then follow and collect the fish that rise to the surface.

There is one more necessary activity—a day devoted to ceremonial labor in the chief's fields. Only then does the drinking begin, and when it does, there is usually non-stop drinking and dancing for five days and nights. The Apalaí are able to consume enormous quantities of their festival drink by regurgitating after every bowlful.

And after five days and nights, the community center runs full with creeks of soured manioc drink.

As the Koehns watched from the sidelines and talked with visiting Apalaí from other villages, they learned the news of what had happened since the last festival.

"Yanari has died of pneumonia." (His name was whispered for a year for fear his spirit might hear it.)

"Poponi, who now has five years, is learning the rhythms of the festival dances."

"Martinta has died. She was poisoned by a jealous woman."

They learned about others who had died from dysentery, pneumonia and malaria.

"Two more babies would have died," said another, "if it had not been for your medicines."

And all the while, Sally and Ed continued to observe. They watched the Apalaí dance, drink, eat and tell stories—mostly of sadness. They heard weeping and screaming as fathers stole their sons from wives of former marriages to take back to work in their fields. There were clashes and fights as men tried to steal others' wives. As they watched, the Koehns realized the Apalaí had little reason for happiness and expressed little joy. They longed to share the good news of another party—the marriage supper of the Lamb. The opportunity came when a young Apalaí man, Azuma, drunk from imbibing gallons and gallons of the manioc drink, fell from a canoe while trying to negotiate some treacherous rapids.

After a quick search, Azuma's brother found him and pulled him out of the water. But since he himself was drunk, he simply plopped Azuma in the bottom of the canoe and left him there. Several hours later when Azuma had not stirred, his brother, panic-stricken, brought him to Ed. For an hour Ed bent over Azuma praying and administering artificial respiration, until finally, Azuma began to breathe.

Later that night as Azuma slept in his hammock, Ed spoke to Azuma's father who was also the local medicine man. Ed told of the greatness of Jesus Christ, how he could give a person power to overcome fear and death.

Nothing happened that night, but Ed knew he had planted another seed. Later when the Gospel of Mark was published, and then Acts and other portions of the Old and New Testament, the Apalaí began to say among themselves, "Because of these good words, we see that Jesus Christ is our rightful owner. We therefore should live obeying him." And one by one, as the Apalaí responded to the Lordship of Christ, Ed and Sally looked back to the days of crises and thanked God for the spiritual groundwork that had been prepared.

Once when the Koehns were out of the village, they received a letter that told them that the Apalaí were in fact appropriating for themselves, albeit painfully, the good news that faith in Christ gives assurance and hope beyond time and space.

Dear Auntie,
There is a lot of sickness in Bona which is whooping cough. Because of this my daughter, who had only 15 days, died. But I know God cares for me truly. I know he wants to teach me things I yet do not understand. I am lonesome for my baby but I will not stop saying thank you to You, Father God, because I know You are good. Therefore I know You have taken her to be with You.

In a way quite apart from the Koehns' personal influence or teaching, the Apalaí, after careful reading of the translated Scriptures, began to not only allow the Holy Spirit to comfort them in moments of bereavement, but also correct their lives. This suddenly dawned on Sally one day when a twenty-seven-year-old woman came to talk with her.

"Mother," said the woman, "God's Spirit has been speaking to me in my insides. I've got to tell you something. Do you remember the time you made a cake and left it on the table and went out of the house? Well, I saw you leave and when you were gone, I went in and saw that cake, and I took a bite and tasted it. Then I didn't know what it was. I knew only that it was good and I tasted some more.

"Then my cousin came in and he asked me what it was I was eating. I told him I didn't know, but it was sure good. Then he tried some and liked it, so he took some more. Then we looked at it and realized we had made a big dent in it.

"At first we didn't know what to do, but then we decided to scratch it all up to make it look like a cat had eaten it. When you came back you said, 'Oh that cat has been into my cake!' Oh, Mother, it wasn't that cat. It was me.

"Also, Little Mother, there was a time when we got into your peanut butter, and once when we took some candy. Oh, Mother, God has been speaking to me in my insides about this and I wonder if I can make you a necklace to pay for these things."

With a wide-open smile, Sally threw her arms around

the woman and said, "Oh, Little Daughter, I love you.
And I am so happy that you are listening to God's Spirit.
You don't have to pay me. Just keep on obeying God."

As the Apalaí applied the Scriptures to their everyday
lives, they found a greater freedom to confess their sins
and become freed from guilt. Quietly, Ed and Sally
savored this practical outworking of the power of the
Gospel. But one day Ed found this freedom to grow and
expand and make things right with a brother could cut
both ways.

For several years, Jacques, a strong handsome
barrel-chested Apalaí, had worked closely with Ed as
together they translated the New Testament. As the
years passed, Ed had helped Jacques develop a small
store. He showed Jacques how to reinvest his profits, to
buy more stock, to anticipate his needs and generally set
Jacques up as a self-supporting merchant.

This was the kind of project, along with establishing a
saw mill and introducing range cattle, that appealed to
Ed's outdoor temperament. Ed was also pleased because
he knew Brazil's proposed North Rim road would
eventually open up Apalaí country. He felt his community development programs would prepare the Apalaí
to meet the onslaught of "civilization."

A beautiful rapport developed between Jacques and
Ed, or so Ed thought. Ed saw evidence of spiritual
growth in Jacques' life. His interest in the Word went
beyond his job of interpreting Scripture to meet the
needs of the Apalaí. Yet with all his spiritual understanding and knowledge, Jacques had not assumed

leadership in the young Apalaí church. And then one
day Ed found out why.

"Eduardo," said Jacques, "I have been saying bad
things about you. And the reason is this. I have a grudge
against you."

"Jacques," said Ed, "I'm sorry. Why is it that you have
a grudge against me?"

"My grudge came when we worked those long days in
Belém," said Jaques.

"I don't understand," said Ed. "Please explain what
happened."

"You told me we would work each day from eight to
five," said Jacques. "But many days you did not stop at
the hour we agreed upon. You would work until 5:30 or
six and never once were you aware we had worked
longer than what we agreed. If you had been aware and
paid me extra for this time I was away from my wife and
family, it would not have bothered me. But since you
were not aware of what you had done, I was bitter."

"What did you do with your bitterness?" asked Ed.

"When I returned to Bona I began to spread false
stories," said Jacques. "I would say to the men of the
village, 'Eduardo doesn't seem to be too happy these
days.' And the other person would say, 'Well, you know
what that is a sign of. He's probably living with another
man's wife.' And I would say, 'Maybe so. Could be. You
are probably right.' "

As the full weight of his insensitivity fell over him, Ed
stretched out his hands and said, "Oh, Jacques, please
forgive me."

"All is forgiven, my brother." said Jacques, "because I too need forgiveness for these false stories and for something else.

"Many years ago my cousin and I worked for a company of Brazilian rubber hunters. The Brazilians accused us of stealing and took us to the police delegation. There I lied. 'We are Indians,' I said. 'When we want rubber we go into the jungle and find it ourselves.' The police let us off, but it wasn't true. We had stolen the rubber blocks and sold them.

"Now that man from whom I stole the rubber is probably dead. But somewhere he must have a widow. Maybe I could pay her something for this debt."

As Ed sat and listened to Jacques, he learned why he and the other Apalaí felt their traditional view of life was no longer adequate to express what they felt the Holy Spirit was teaching them.

"Do you remember, Brother Eduardo, when we were struggling hard to find words in Apalaí for the parts of the tabernacle?" said Jacques. "Words like 'mercy seat,' 'candlestick,' 'Holy of Holies,' and I asked you if God had a place like this today, and you said no. Then do you remember you showed me pictures of what the tabernacle was like.

"As I thought about this, I began to see that God still has a place like this. He no longer dwells in a building called a temple, but he does dwell in our insides. And because he tells me my body is a temple in which he dwells, I want my insides to be clean. It is for this reason I have come to ask your forgiveness and the forgiveness of all I have offended."

As Ed sat munching some freshly-made brownies Sally had made in her mud stove, he thought about all the Lord had done during their thirteen years in Bona.

"I've been thinking, honey." said Ed to Sally, "Now that the New Testament is almost complete and there are several Apalaí who regularly prepare Bible studies, I feel I can start 'taking in' as well as 'giving out.' I no longer feel that tremendous weight that I am the only one in all the world responsible for the spiritual well-being of the Apalaí. I now have Apalaí Christian brothers who have assumed this as their responsibility before the Lord."

Sally, brushing tears from her cheeks, nodded her head in wistful agreement. She recalled an incident that had happened a few weeks before. She had been alone in the village on Sunday and asked if the believers would like to meet in her home for a reading.

She chose Genesis 3, talked about the prophecy of Christ, then turned to the New Testament to show how the Scriptures tied together. When the reading was over, Sally asked Jacques to pray.

"Father up in the skies," prayed Jacques, "thank You that we are just beginning to have your Word. Thank You for sending my Uncle Eduardo, my Aunt Sally to give us your Words. If they had not come to love us and teach us, we would not have had your Words. Thank You for sending them."

Sally had never heard such a beautiful prayer, and she wept. She wept remembering their first months among the Apalaí and how hard she thought it was to live in such an impossible place, among such a horrid people.

And then Sally prayed. "O God," she cried, "how could I have ever felt like that? How gracious You are. How beautiful You have been to allow us the privilege of giving away a little of what You have given us. And thank You, Lord, for giving us the strength to plant a seed and 'run with the footmen.'"

Chapter 12

Hello to you, my brothers and sisters. You have just read about Eduardo and Sally and how I pray and thank our Heavenly Father for sending them such a great distance to come and love us and teach us about God. Let me therefore explain in my own words just how it was that I came to believe in Jesus and to trust Him as my Genuine Owner.

Long ago when I was a child, I didn't know Jesus. I didn't know God. I just believed in the earth, sky and water. I did not think about where these had come from and since I did not know the Creator, I thought all these things just happened by themselves.

As a child I was unhappy most of the time. My mother had no real husband and wanted to kill me when I was born. But my grandmother saved me from being clubbed and buried in the ground.

When I grew up, I married. And I did a lot of bad things. I got drunk. I became angry and said nasty things about others. I said I loved my relatives, but it was just talk. In my insides I knew I didn't care for them at all. I was selfish. When they would come to visit, I wished they would leave.

After a while I took my wife and baby to a river in Surinam where a person lived who said he knew about

God. This man spoke my language and invited me to study and believe in Jesus as my Genuine Owner.

I didn't know who Jesus was, and when they said, "Receive him," I didn't understand. "Yes, I receive him," I said, but I kept doing bad things because I really didn't understand. I was still ignorant when I returned to Bona and the Paru River.

Then God sent Ed and Sally to us to teach us and to love us. As I think about it, I wonder what would have happened to us if they had not come and taught us about Jesus. We had lots of visitors on the Paru River—rubber hunters, seekers for gold and jaguar—but no one told us about the Lord. What they taught us was something else—killing, stealing, adultery, how to do wrong things.

One day an Indian friend—a Christian—came to visit me from another place. His name was Jaco and he told me that it was important for me to believe in Jesus.

I listened, skeptically. I had learned to read. I owned a copy of the Gospel of Mark and Acts that Eduardo had translated and I knew some songs. I told Jaco, "I am believing, but I don't understand completely."

As Jaco talked to me I asked him how it was that he did not carouse with other women. I thought it was probably his wife's jealousy that made him leave other women alone.

Then one day I believed in Jesus and Jaco urged me to tell my teacher, Eduardo. My wife also decided to take Jesus as her Genuine Owner, but our faith was very weak. Sin tempted me more than ever.

The sin that attracted me most was adultery. It was like a sickness the way I carried on. But then something happened. I learned that my wife had been unfaithful to me. Now I was presented with a problem. How was I to react as a Christian? I was deeply hurt. I wanted to make the offender pay for his sin—maybe even kill him.

But then I began to reflect on my own condition. I had been guilty of the same sin many times over. I wondered how I could appease God. If I could pay for my sin, what did I have that would make such a payment? The only payment was the death of Jesus. When I understood this, I put my whole trust in Jesus and let go of my sin.

When I did that, no one could accuse me any longer. Neither could they take advantage of my wife because she also believed in Jesus as her Lord. He became *our Lord*.

What about the hurt I had caused when I messed with other men's wives? There was plenty of hurt that I had caused before I believed. To be occupied with women was a pleasure to me, but to have others mess with my wife was very painful.

Little by little I began to understand that just as the sin of others caused me great pain, so my sin caused pain to others and to the Lord our Owner. Thus, now that I love the Lord, I want to care for others. I don't want to cause them pain.

Now I am not so preoccupied with other women. I still have temptations, but since I know the Lord, I quickly trust him for the power to resist. This is what the believers say I should do, and it works!

At first I didn't understand how this would work. Then I watched those who were believers in Jesus and listened to what they said. I saw how Eduardo and Sally had left home and relatives to bring us God's Word, and seeing this I wanted to be obedient, not just to man, but to God.

Before, if a man said, "Leave your sins. Don't mess with women," my response was silence. In my heart I said, "You're not God." But now I will listen and obey because God has spoken. I am happy now because I recognize his strength. When I get sick, I'm still happy about Jesus. If I should get lost while I am hunting, I would still be happy.

My life is now so different. I used to be constantly on the go, not sleeping at nights, thinking about other women. I didn't like work. I was lazy. I was occupied with my sin. But now there has been a change. I am no longer filled with fears and guilt. I am at peace and unworried. I am glad for this because this is the way I want my life to be—obedient to the Lord who is my Genuine Owner.

Now I understand that Jesus is the Creator and Owner of all things. Nothing is too hard for God. Therefore, let us all obey him. He loves us. When we are ugly, or sinful, or bad, he still loves us.

Now I want to teach my wife and my children and others more about him. I want them to follow God. When God tells me to go, I want to obey, and therefore I must go to other villages and teach them about the Lord.

This is all I want to say except I want to tell you once again that I am happy. I know the Lord.